WHITE BEAR LAKE.

THE

SEAT OF EMPIRE.

BY

CHARLES CARLETON COFFIN,

"CARLETON."

"I now believe that the ultimate last seat of government on this great continent will be found somewhere within a circle or radius not very far from the spot on which I stand, at the head of navigation on the Mississippi River."

W. H. SEWARD, *Speech at St. Paul*, 1860.

BOSTON:
FIELDS, OSGOOD, & CO.
1870.

UNIVERSITY PRESS: WELCH, BIGELOW, & CO.,
CAMBRIDGE.

TO

JOHN GREGORY SMITH,

GOVERNOR OF VERMONT DURING THE REBELLION,

WHOM I FIRST SAW TENDERLY CARING FOR THE SICK AND WOUNDED IN THE HOSPITALS OF FREDERICKSBURG, AND THROUGH WHOSE ENERGY AND PERSEVERANCE ONE OF THE GREATEST ENTERPRISES OF THE PRESENT CENTURY HAS BEEN SUCCESSFULLY INAUGURATED,

This Volume

IS AFFECTIONATELY INSCRIBED.

CONTENTS.

CHAPTER I.

FROM CHICAGO TO MINNEAPOLIS.

CHAPTER II.

ST. CLOUD AND BEYOND.

CHAPTER III.

THE RED RIVER COUNTRY.

CHAPTER IV.

THE EMPIRE OF THE NORTHWEST.

CHAPTER V.

THE FRONTIER.

CHAPTER VI.

ROUND THE CAMP-FIRE.

CHAPTER VII.

IN THE FOREST.

CHAPTER VIII.

DULUTH.

CHAPTER IX.

THE MINING REGION.

CHAPTER X.

A FAMILIAR TALK.

CHAPTER XI.

NORTHERN PACIFIC RAILROAD.

THE SEAT OF EMPIRE.

CHAPTER I.

FROM CHICAGO TO MINNEAPOLIS.

LAST summer I cut loose from all care, and enjoyed a few weeks of freedom and recreation with a party of gentlemen on the frontier between Lake Superior and the Missouri River. I was charmed by the beauty of the country, amazed at its resources, and favorably impressed by its probable future. Its attractions were set forth in a series of letters contributed to the Boston Journal.

People from every Eastern State, as well as from New York and the British Provinces, have called upon me since my return, for the purpose of "having a talk about the Northwest," while others have applied by letter for additional or specific information, and others still have requested a republication of the letters. In response to these calls this small volume has been prepared, setting forth the physical features of the vast reach of country lying between the Lakes and the Pacific, not only in the United States, but in British America as well.

The most trustworthy accounts of persons who have lived there, as well as of engineers who have been sent out by the United States, British, and Canadian governments, have been collated, that those seeking a home in Minnesota or Dakota may know what sort of a country lies beyond, and what will be its probable future.

The map accompanying the volume has been prepared for the most part by the Bureau of the United States Topographical Engineers. It gives me pleasure to acknowledge my indebtedness to Major-General Humphreys, in charge of the Bureau, and to Colonel Woodruffe, in charge of the map department, for permission to use the same.

Through their courtesy I am enabled to place before the public the most complete map ever published of the country between the 36th and 55th parallel, extending across the continent, and showing not only the entire railway system of the Eastern and Middle States, but also the Union Pacific Railroad and the Northern Pacific, now under construction. The figures followed by the letter T have reference to the elevation of the locality above tide-water, thus enabling the reader to obtain at a glance a comprehensive idea of the topographical as well as the geographical features of the country.

"All aboard for the Northwest!"

So shouted the stalwart porter of the Sherman House, Chicago, on the morning of the 5th of July, 1869.

Giving heed to the call, we descended the steps of the hotel and entered an omnibus waiting at the door, that quickly whirled us to the depot of the Chicago and Northwestern Railroad.

There were about a dozen gentlemen in the party, all bound for the Northwest, to explore a portion of the vast reach of country lying between Lake Superior and the great northern bend of the Missouri River.

It was a pleasant, sunny, joyful morning. The anniversary of the nation's independence having fallen on the Sabbath, the celebration was observed on Monday, and the streets resounded with the explosion of fire-crackers. Americans, Germans, Norwegians, Irish, people of all nationalities, were celebrating the birthday of their adopted country. Not only in Chicago, but throughout the cosmopolitan State of Wisconsin, as we sped over its fertile prairies and through its towns and villages during the day, there was a repetition of the scene.

Settlers from New England and the Middle States were having Sabbath-School, temperance, or civic celebrations; Irish societies were marching in procession, bearing green banners emblazoned with the shamrock, thistle, and harp of Erin; Germans were drinking lager beer, singing songs, and smoking their meerschaums. All work was laid aside, and all hands — farmers with their wives and daughters, young men with their sweethearts, children in crowds — were observing in their various ways the return of the holiday.

Our route was by way of La Crosse, which we reached late in the evening. We were to go up the Mississippi on a steamer that lay moored to the bank. Its cabin was aglow with lights. Entering it, we found a party of ladies and gentlemen formed for a quadrille. They were the officers of the boat and their friends from the town. A negro with a bass-viol, and two Germans with violins, were tuning their instruments and rosining their bows.

We were met upon the threshold by a rosy-cheeked damsel, who gleefully exclaimed, —

" O, yeau have arrived at the right moment! We are having a right good time, and we only want one more gentleman to make it go real good. Yeau 'll dance neaw, won't ye? I want a partner. O, ye will neaw. I know ye will, and ye 'll call off the changes tew, won't ye? Neaw dew."

Not having a "light fantastic toe" on either foot, we were forced to say no to this lively La Crosse maiden; besides, we were tired and covered with dust, and in sad plight for the ball-room.

A member of Congress was next appealed to, then a grave and dignified Doctor of Divinity.

A more ungallant party than ours never stood on a Western steamboat. Governor, judge, parson, members of Congress, all shook their heads and resisted the enthusiastic lady. In vain she urged them, and the poor girl, with downcast countenance, turned from the obdurate Yankees, and sailed in gloriously with a youth who fortunately entered the cabin at the moment.

It was a rare sight to see, for they danced with a will. They made the steamer shake from stem to stern. The glass lamps tinkled in their brass settings, and the doors of staterooms rattled on their hinges, especially when the largest gentleman of the party came to a shuffle.

He is the Daniel Lambert of the Mississippi,—immense and gigantic, and having great development round the equator.

Quadrille, cotillon, and waltz, and genuine western break-downs followed one after the other. There was plenty to eat and drink in the pantry. The first thing we heard in the evening was the tuning of the instruments; the last thing, as we dropped off to sleep, was the scraping of the violins and the shuffling of feet.

We are awake in the morning in season to take a look at the place before the boat casts off from its mooring for a trip to Winona.

A company of Norwegian emigrants that came with us on the train from Chicago are cooking their breakfast in and around the station. They sailed from Christiania for Quebec, and have been six weeks on the way. All ages are represented. It is a party made up of families. There are many light-haired maidens among them with deep blue eyes and blonde complexions; and robust young men with honest faces, who have bidden farewell forever to their old homes upon the fiords of Norway, and who henceforth are to be citizens of the United States.

They will find immediate employment on the railroads of Minnesota, in the construction of new lines. They are not hired by the day, but small sections are let out to individuals, who receive a specified sum for every square yard of earth thrown up.

There is no discussion of the eight-hour question among them. They work sixteen hours of their own accord, instead of haggling over eight. They have no time to engage in rows, nor do they find occasion. They have had a bare existence in their old home; life there was ever a struggle, the mere keeping together of soul and body, but here Hope leads them on. They are poor now, but a few years hence they will be well off in the world. They will have farms, nice houses, money in banks, government bonds, and railway stocks. They will obtain land at government price, will raise wheat, wool, or stock, and will soon find their land quadrupled in value. They will make excellent citizens. Their hearts are on the right side, — not physiologically, but morally, politically, and religiously speaking. They are ardent lovers of liberty; they cannot be trammelled by any shackles, political or ecclesiastical. They are frugal, industrious, and honest. Already there are several daily papers published in the Scandinavian language.

The steamer is ploughing the Mississippi against the current northward. Wisconsin is on our right, Minnesota on our left; and while we are moving on toward the region of country which we are to visit, we may while away the time by thinking over the general characteristics of the State of Minnesota, in which our explorations are to commence.

The southern boundary strikes the river twenty-two miles below La Crosse. If I were to go down there and turn my steps due west, I might walk two hundred and sixty-four miles along the Iowa line before reaching the southwestern corner of the State. The western side is the longest, and if I were to start from the southwestern corner and travel due north, I should have a journey of three hundred and sixty miles to accomplish before reaching the northern boundary, —

the line between the United States and British America.

Starting from Pembina, at the northwest corner of the State, on the Red River of the North, and travelling due east eighty miles, I should reach the Lake of the Woods; sailing across it sixty miles, then entering the river leading to Rainy Lake, I might pass through the wonderful waterway of lakes and rivers reaching to Lake Superior, — a distance of about four hundred miles.

The eastern boundary formed by the Mississippi, St. Croix, and Lake Superior is more irregular. Its general outline, as we look at it upon the map, is that of a crescent, cutting into Minnesota, the horns turned eastward. The area within the boundaries thus described is estimated at 84,000 square miles, or 54,760,000 acres. It is a territory larger than Maine, New Hampshire, Vermont, Massachusetts, Rhode Island, and Connecticut combined.

Here, upon the Mississippi, I gaze upon bluffs of gray limestone wrought into fantastic shape by the winds and storms of centuries and by the slow wearing of the river; but were I to climb them, and gain the general level of the country, I should behold rolling prairies dotted with lakes and ponds of pure water, and groves of oak and hickory. All of Minnesota east of the Mississippi is a timbered region. Here and there are openings; but, speaking in general terms, the entire country east of the river is a forest, which through the coming years will resound with the axe of the lumberman.

When we go up the Mississippi eighty miles above St. Paul to St. Cloud, we shall find the Sauk River coming in from the west; and there the Mississippi is no longer the boundary of the timbered lands, but the forest reaches across the stream westward to Otter-Tail River, a distance of more than one hundred miles. The Sauk River is its southern boundary.

All the region north of the Sauk, at the headwaters of the Mississippi and north of Lake Superior, is well supplied with timber. A belt of woods forty miles wide, starting from the Crow-Wing River, extends south nearly to the Iowa boundary. It is broken here and there by prairie openings and fertile meadows. The tract is known throughout the Northwest as the region of the "Big Woods."

There are fringes of timber along the streams, so that the settler, wherever he may wish to make a home, will generally find material for building purposes within easy reach. In this respect Minnesota is one of the most favored States of the Union.

The formations of the bluffs now and then remind us of old castles upon the Rhine. They are, upon an average, three hundred and fifty feet above the summer level of the river. We are far from the Gulf of Mexico, yet the river at St. Paul is only six hundred and seventy-six feet above tide-water.

Northward of Minneapolis the bluffs disappear, and the surface of the river is but a few feet below the general level of the country, which is about one thousand feet above the sea.

It is one of the remarkable topographical features of the continent, that from St. Paul to the Peace River, which empties into the Athabasca, the elevation is about the same, though the distance is more than one thousand miles. Throughout this great extent of territory, especially in Minnesota, are innumerable lakes and ponds of pure fresh water, some of them having no visible outlet or inlet, with pebbly shores and beaches of white sand, bordered by groves and parks of oak, ash, and maple, lending an indescribable charm to the beauty of the landscape.

While we are making these observations the steamer is nearing Winona, a pleasant town, delightfully situated on a low prairie, elevated but a few feet above the river. The bluffs at this point recede, giving ample room for a town site with a ravine behind it.

Nature has done a great deal for the place, — scooping out the ravine as if the sole purpose had been to make the construction of a railroad an easy matter. The Winona and St. Peter's Railway strikes out from the town over the prairie, winds through the ravine, and by easy grades gains the rolling country beyond. The road is nearly completed to the Minnesota River, one hundred and forty miles. It will eventually be extended to the western boundary of the State, and onward into Dakota. It is now owned by the Chicago and Northwestern Railway Company, and runs through the centre of the second tier of counties in the State. The Southern Minnesota Railroad starts from La Crosse, and runs west through the first tier of counties. It is already constructed half-way across the State, and will be pushed on, as civilization advances, to the Missouri. That is the objective point of all the lines of railway leading west from the Mississippi, and they will soon be there.

This city of Winona fifteen years ago had about one hundred inhabitants. It was a place where steamers stopped to take wood and discharge a few packages of freight, but to-day it has a population of nine thousand. Looking out upon it from the promenade deck of the steamer, we see new buildings going up, and can hear the hammers and saws of the carpenters. It already contains thirteen churches and a Normal School with three hundred scholars, who are preparing to teach the children of the State, though the probabilities are that most of them will soon teach their own offspring instead of their neighbors'; for in the West young men are plenty, maidens scarce. Out here —

> "There is no goose so gray but soon or late
> Will find some honest gander for her mate."

Not so in the East, for the young men there are pushing west, and women are in the majority. It is a certainty that some of them will know more of single blessedness than of married life. If they would only come out here, the certainty would be the other way.

Not stopping at Winona, but hastening on board the train, we fly over the prairie, up the ravine, and out through one of the most fertile sections of the great grain-field of the Northwest.

The superintendent of the road, Mr. Stewart, accompanies our party, and we receive pleasure and profit by having a gentleman with us who is so thoroughly informed as he to point out the objects of interest along the way. By a winding road, now running under a high bluff where the limestone ledges overhang the track, now gliding over a high trestle-bridge from the northern to the southern side of the deep ravine, we gain at length the general table-land, and behold, reaching as far as the eye can see, fields of wheat. Fences are visible here and there, showing the division of farms; but there is scarcely a break in the sea of grain, in flower now, rippling and waving in the passing breeze. Farm-houses dot the landscape, and white cottages are embowered in surrounding groves, and here and there we detect a small patch of corn or an acre of potatoes, — small islands these in the great ocean of wheat reaching westward, northward, and southward.

We are astonished when the train nears St. Charles, a town of two thousand inhabitants, looking marvellously like a New England village, to see a school-house just completed at a cost of $15,000! and still wider open we our eyes at Rochester, with a population of six thousand, where we behold a school-building that has cost $60,000! Upon inquiry we ascertain that the bulk of the population of these towns is from New England.

A ride of about ninety miles brings us to Owatona, a town of about three thousand inhabitants.

We are in Steele County. The little rivulets here meandering through the prairie and flowing southward reach the Mississippi only after crossing the State of Iowa, while those running northward join the Mississippi through the Minnesota River.

Here, as at Rochester, we behold charming landscapes, immense fields of grain, groves of trees, snug cottages and farm-houses, and a thrifty town. Owatona has a school-house that cost the citizens $20,000; yet nine years ago the population of the entire county was only 2,862! The census of

1870 will probably make it 15,000. So civilization advances, not only here, but all through the Northwest, especially where there are railroad facilities.

From Owatona we turn north and pass through Rice County, containing eighteen townships. It is one of the best-timbered counties west of the Mississippi; there are large tracts of oak, maple, butternut, walnut, poplar, elm, and boxwood. We glide through belts of timber where choppers are felling the trees for railroad ties, past fields where the industrious husbandman has turned the natural grasses of the prairie into blooming clover.

At Faribault a company of Norwegians, recently arrived from their homes beyond the sea, and not having reached their journey's end, are cooking their supper near the station. To-morrow they will be pushing on westward to the grounds already purchased by the agent who has brought them out.

In 1850 this entire county had only one hundred inhabitants; the census of next year will probably show a population of twenty-five thousand, — one half Americans, one sixth Germans, one ninth Irish, besides Norwegians, Swedes, and Canadians. Faribault has about four thousand inhabitants, who have laid excellent foundations for future growth. They have an Episcopal College, a High School for ladies, a Theological Seminary, a Deaf and Dumb Asylum, two Congregational churches, also one Baptist, one Methodist, and one Episcopal. They have excellent water-power on the Cannon River. Five flouring-mills have already been erected.

Fourteen miles beyond this place we find Northfield with three thousand inhabitants, three fourths of them New-Englanders. Five churches and a college, two flouring-mills capable of turning out one hundred thousand barrels per annum, excellent schools, a go-ahead population, are the characteristics of this thoroughly wide-awake town.

A mile or two beyond Northfield we enter Dakota County, — one of the most fertile in the State. It was one of the first settled, and in 1860 contained 9,058 inhabitants. Its present population is estimated at 20,000, — one third of them Irish, one third Americans, one quarter Germans, and the remainder of all nationalities. The largest town is Hastings, on the Mississippi, containing about four thousand inhabitants. The Hastings and Dakota Railroad, extending west, crosses the Milwaukie and St. Paul at Farmington, a pleasant little town located on a green and fertile prairie. Thirty miles of this Hastings and Dakota road are in operation, and it is pushing on westward, like all the others, to reach the territory of Dakota and the Missouri River.

On over the prairies we fly, reaching the oldest

town in the State, Mendota, which was a trading-post of the American Fur Company as long ago as 1828. It was livelier then than now, for in those years Indians by the thousand made it their rendezvous, coming in their bark canoes down the Minnesota from the borders of Dakota, down the St. Croix, which joins the Mississippi opposite Hastings, down the Mississippi from all the region above the Falls of St. Anthony; but now it is a seedy place. The houses have a forlorn look, and the three hundred Irish and Germans that make up the bulk of the population are not of the class that lay the foundations of empires, or make the wilderness bud and blossom with roses; they take life easy, and let to-day wait on to-morrow.

Fort Snelling, admirably located, looms grandly above the high steep bluff of the northern bank of the Minnesota River. It was one of the strongest posts on the frontier, but it is as useless now as a last year's swallow's-nest. The frontier is three hundred miles farther on.

Upon the early maps of Minnesota I find a magnificent city occupying the surrounding ground. It was surveyed and plotted, but St. Paul and Minneapolis got ahead, and the city of Snelling has no place in history.

We approach St. Paul from the south. Stepping from the cars we find ourselves on the lowlands of the Mississippi, with a high bluff south of us, and another on the north bank, both rising perpendicularly from the river. We ride over a long wooden bridge, one end of which rests on the low land by the railroad station, and the other on the high northern bluff, so that the structure is inclined at an angle of about twenty degrees, like the driveway to a New England barn where the floor is nearly up to the high beams. We are in a city which in 1849, twenty years ago, had a population of eight hundred and forty, but which now has an estimated population of twenty-five thousand. Here that powerful tribe of Northern Indians, the Dakotas, had their capital, — a cave in the sandstone bluffs, which was the council-chamber of the tribe. Upon the bluff now stands the capital of the State, and the sanguine citizens believe that the city is to be the commercial metropolis of the Northwest. A few months ago I was on the other side of the globe, where civilization is at a standstill; where communities exist, but scarcely change; where decay is quite as probable as growth; where advancement is the exception, and not the rule. To ride through the streets of St. Paul; to behold its spacious warehouses, its elegant edifices, stores piled with the goods of all lands, the products of all climes, — furs from Hudson Bay, oranges from Messina, teas from China, coffee from Brazil, silks from Paris, and all the products of industry from our own land; to behold the streets alive with people, crowded with farmers' wagons laden with wheat and flour; to read the signs, "Young Men's Christian Association," "St. Paul Library Association"; to see elegant school-edifices and churches, beautiful private residences surrounded by lawns and adorned with works of art, — to see this in contrast with what we have so lately witnessed, and to think that this is the development of American civilization, going on now as never before, and destined to continue till all this wide region is to be thus dotted over with centres of influence and power, sends an indescribable thrill through our veins. It is not merely that we are Americans, but because in this land Christian civilization is attaining the highest development of all time. The people of St. Paul may justly take pride in what they have already accomplished, and they also have reason to look forward with confidence to the future.

The county is quite small, containing only four and a half townships. The soil is poor, a sandy loam, of not much account for farming purposes, but being at the head of steamboat navigation a good start was obtained; and now that railroads are superseding steamboats, St. Paul reaches out her iron arms in every direction, — up the Mississippi to St. Cloud, westward through Minneapolis to the Red River of the North, southwest to touch the Missouri at Sioux City, due south over the line by which we reached the city, down the river towards Chicago, and northeast to Lake Superior. As a spider extends its threads, so St. Paul, or perhaps, more properly speaking, St. Paul and Minneapolis together, are throwing out their lines of communication, making themselves the centre of the great Northwest systems of railways. The interests of St. Paul are mercantile, those of Minneapolis manufacturing. They are nearly five hundred miles distant from Chicago, — far enough to be an independent commercial, manufacturing, and distributing centre. That such is to be their destiny cannot be doubted.

The outfit of our party had been prepared at Minneapolis; and a large number of gentlemen from that city made their appearance at St. Paul, to convey us to the town in their own private carriages.

It is a charming ride that we have along the eastern bank of the Mississippi, which pours its mighty flood, — mighty even here, though so far away from the sea, — rolling and thundering far below us in the chasm which it has worn in the solid rock.

On our right hand are fields of waving grain, and white cottages half hidden in groves of oak and maple. We see New England thrift and enterprise, for the six States east of the Hudson have been sending their wide-awake sons and daughters to this section for the last twenty years. The gentleman with whom we are riding came here from the woods of Maine, a lumberman from the Penobscot, and has been the architect of his own fortune. He knows all about the Upper Mississippi, its tributaries, and the chain of lakes lying northwest of Lake Superior. He is Mayor of Minneapolis, a substantial citizen, his hand ready for every good work, — for the building of schools and churches, for charity and benevolence; but on the Upper Mississippi he wears a red shirt, eats pork and beans, and sleeps on pine boughs. He directs the labor of hundreds of wood-choppers and raftsmen.

How different this from what we see in other lands! I find my pen runs on contrasts. How can one help it after seeing that gorgeous and lumbering old carriage in which the Lord Mayor of London rides from Guildhall to Westminster? The Lord Mayor himself appears in a scarlet cloak not half so becoming as a red shirt. He wears a massive gold chain, and a hat which would be most in place on the stage of a theatre, and which would make him a guy in any American town. Not so do the Lord Mayors of the Northwest appear in public. They understand practical life. It is one of the characteristics of our democratic government that it makes people practical in all things.

In 1865 the town of Minneapolis contained only 4,607 inhabitants, but the population by the census of the present year is 13,080.

The fall in the river at this point is sixty-four feet, furnishing 120,000 horse-power, — more than sufficient to drive every mill-wheel and factory in New England, and, according to Wheelock's Report, greater than the whole motive-power — steam and water — employed in textile manufactures in England in 1850. Thirteen flouring-mills, fourteen saw-mills, two woollen-mills, and two paper-mills, are already erected. Six million dollars have been invested in manufacturing at this point. The only difficulty to be encountered is the preservation of the falls in their present position. Beneath the slate rock over which the torrent pours is a strata of soft sandstone, which rapidly wears away. Measures have been taken, however, to preserve the cataract in its present condition, by constructing an apron to carry the water some distance beyond the verge of the fall and thus prevent the breaking away of the rock.

No one can behold the natural advantages at Minneapolis without coming to the conclusion that it is to be one of the great manufacturing cities of the world if the fall can be kept in its present position. Cotton can be loaded upon steamers at Memphis, and discharged at St. Paul. The climate here is exceedingly favorable for the manufacturing of cotton goods. The lumber-mills by and by will give place to other manufactures, and Minneapolis will rank with Lowell or Fall River.

Our ride brings us to St. Anthony on the east bank of the river, where we behold the Mississippi roaring and tumbling over the slate-stone ledges, and hear the buzzing and humming of the machinery in the saw-mills.

St. Anthony was one of the earliest-settled towns in the State. Its projectors were Southern men. Streets were laid out, stores erected, a great hotel built, and extravagant prices asked for land, but the owners of Minneapolis offered lots at cheaper rates, and found purchasers. The war came on, and the proprietors of St. Anthony being largely from the South, the place ceased to grow, while its rival on the western shore moved steadily onward in a prosperous career. But St. Anthony is again advancing, for many gentlemen doing business in Minneapolis reside there. The interests of the two places are identical, and will advance together.

How can one describe what is indescribable? I can only speak of this city as situated on a beautiful plain, with the Mississippi thundering over a cataract with a power sufficient to build up half a dozen Lowells; with a country behind it where every acre of land as far as the eye can see, and a hundred or a thousand times farther, is capable of cultivation and of supporting a population as dense as that of Belgium or China. Wide streets, costly school-houses, church spires, a community in which the New England element largely predominates, — a city where every other door does not open to a lager-beer saloon, as in some Western towns; where the sound of the saw and the hammer, and the click of the mason's trowel and sledge, are heard from morning till night; where the streets are filled with wagons from the country, bringing in grain and carrying back lumber, with the farmer, his wife and buxom daughter, and tow-headed, bright-faced little boys perched on top — such are the characteristics of Minneapolis.

There was a time when Pegasus was put in harness, and the ancients, according to fable, tried to put Hercules to work. If those days of classic story have gone by, better ones have come, for the people of Minneapolis have got the Father of Waters in harness. He is cutting out one hundred million feet of lumber per annum here. I can hear him spinning his saws. He is turning a score of millstones, and setting a million or two of spindles in motion, and pretty soon some of the citizens intend to set him to weaving bags and cloth by the hundred thousand yards! Only a tithe of his strength is yet laid out. These men, reared in the East, and developed in the West, will make the old Father work for them henceforth. He will not be allowed to idle away his time by leaping and laughing year in and year out over yonder cataract. He must work for the good of the human race. They will use him for the building of a great mart of industry, — for the erection of houses and homes, the abodes of comfort and happiness and of joyful and peaceful life.

CHAPTER II.

ST. CLOUD AND BEYOND.

ST. CLOUD was the rendezvous of the party, where a grand ovation awaited us, — a band of music at the station, a dinner at the hotel, a ride to Sauk Rapids, two miles above the town.

St. Cloud is eighty miles above St. Paul, situated on the west bank of the river, and is reached by the St. Paul and Pacific Railroad. The goods of the Hudson Bay Company pass through the town. Three hundred tons per annum are shipped from Liverpool to Montreal, from Montreal to Milwaukie, from Milwaukie by rail to this point, and from hence are transported by oxen to the Red River, taken down that stream on a small steamer to Lake Winnipeg, then sent in boats and canoes up the Assinniboin, the Saskatchawan, and to all the numerous trading-posts between Winnipeg and the Arctic Ocean.

We are getting towards the frontier. We come upon frontiersmen in leggings, slouch hat, and fur coat, — carrying their rifles. Indians are riding their ponies. Wigwams are seen in the groves. Carts are here from Pembina and Fort Garry after supplies.

And yet, in the suburbs of the town we see a large Normal School building just completed. A magnificent bridge costing $40,000 spans the Mississippi. At Sauk Rapids the river rolls over a granite ledge, and a chartered water-power company is erecting a dam, constructing a canal, and laying the foundations for the second great manufacturing city upon the Mississippi.

This section has been a favorite locality for German emigrants. Nearly one half of the inhabitants of Stearns County, of which St. Cloud is the county-seat, are Germans. Here we bid good by to the locomotive and take the saddle instead, with light carriages for occasional change.

We leave hotels behind, and are to enjoy the pleasures of camp-life.

Our party as made up consists of the following persons: —

Gov. J. Gregory Smith, St. Albans, Vt.
W. C. Smith, M. C. " "
W. H. Lord, D. D., Montpelier, Vt.
F. E. Woodbridge, Vergennes, Vt.
S. W. Thayer, M. D., Burlington, Vt.
Hon. R. D. Rice, Augusta, Me.
P. Coburn, " "
E. F. Johnson, Middletown, Conn.
C. C. Coffin, Boston.
P. W. Holmes, New York City.
A. B. Bayless, Jr., New York City.
W. R. Marshall, St. Paul, Gov. of Minnesota.
E. M. Wilson, M. C., Minneapolis.
G. A. Brackett, "

The list is-headed by Ex-Governor Smith, President of the Northern Pacific Railroad and of the Vermont Central. It fell to his lot to be Chief Magistrate of the Green Mountain State during the rebellion, and among all the loyal governors there was no one that excelled him in energy and executive force. He was here, there, and everywhere, — one day in Vermont, the next in Washington, the third in the rear of the army looking after the wounded. I remember seeing him at Fredericksburg during those terrible weeks that followed the struggles at the Wilderness and Spottsylvania, — directing his assistants, laboring with his own hands, — hunting up the sick and wounded, giving up his own cot, sleeping on the bare floor, or not sleeping at all, — cheering the despondent, writing sympathetic letters to fathers and mothers whose sons were in the hospital, or who had given their lives to their country. He has taken hold of this great enterprise — the construction of a railroad across the continent from the Lakes to the Pacific Ocean — with like zeal and energy, and has organized this expedition to explore the country between Lake Superior and the Missouri River.

Judge Rice is from Maine. He is President of the Portland and Kennebec Railroad, and a director of the Northern Pacific. Before engaging in the management of railroads he held, for sixteen years, the honorable and responsible position of Associate Judge of the Supreme Court of Maine. Well versed in law, and holding the scales of justice evenly, his decisions have been regarded as wise and just.

Mr. Johnson is the Chief Engineer of the road, one of the ablest in his profession in the country. As long ago as 1853, before the government surveys were made, he published a pamphlet upon this future highway to the Pacific, in which he discussed with great ability the physical geography of the country, not only from Lake Superior to Puget Sound, but the entire region between the Mississippi and the Pacific. The explorations that have since been made correspond almost exactly with his statements.

The President of the company has showed forethought for the health, comfort, and pleasure of the party, by taking along two of the most genial men in New England, — Dr. Thayer, of Burlington, to cure us of all the ills that flesh is heir to, whose broad smiling face is itself a most excellent medicine, whose stories are quite as good as his pills and powders for keeping our digestion all right; and Rev. Dr. Lord, from Montpelier, for many years pastor of one of the largest churches in the State.

With a doctor to keep our bodies right, with a minister to point out the narrow way that leads to a brighter world, and both of them as warm-hearted and genial as sunshine, we surely ought to be in good health.

Mr. Holmes, of New York, is an old campaigner. He had experienced the rough and tumble of life on the Upper Missouri, with his rifle for a companion, the earth his bed, the broad expanse of sky his tent.

Governor Marshall, Chief Magistrate of Minnesota, Mr. Wilson, member of Congress from the same State, and Mr. Brackett, of Minneapolis, were in Sibley's expedition against the Indians, and are accustomed to all the pleasures and hardships of a campaign. They are to explore the region lying between the Red River of the North and the Great Bend of the Missouri. Mr. Bayless, of New York, accompanies the party to enjoy the freedom and excitement of frontier life. Nor are we without other company. Some of the clergymen of Minnesota, like their brethren in other parts of the country, turn their backs on civilization during the summer months, and spend a few weeks with Nature for a teacher. It is related that the Rev. Dr. Bethune made it a point to visit Moosehead Lake in Maine every season, to meditate in solitude and eat onions! He not only loved them, but had great faith in their strengthening powers. His ministry was a perpetual Lent so far as onions were concerned, and it was only when he broke away from society and was lost to the world in the forest that he could partake freely of his favorite vegetable.

Travelling the same road, and keeping us company, are Rev. Mr. and Mrs. Fuller, of Rochester, and Rev. Mr. and Mrs. Williams, and Mr. and Miss Wheaton, of Northfield, Minn. They have a prairie wagon with a covered top, drawn by two horses, in which is packed a tent, with pots, kettles, pans, dishes, flour, pork, beans, canned fruit, hams, butter, bed and bedding. They have saddle-horses for excursions, and carry rifles, shot-guns, and fishing-tackle. Pulpit, people and parsonage, hoop-skirts, stove-pipe hats, work and care, are left behind. The women can handle the fishing-rod or rifle. It may seem to ladies unaccustomed to country life as a great letting down of dignity on the part of these women of the West to enter upon such an expedition, but they are in search of health. They are not aiming to be Amazons. A few weeks upon the prairies, and they will return well browned, but healthful and rugged, and as attractive and charming as the fair Maud who raked hay and dreamed of what might have been.

Our first night is spent at "Camp Thunder," and why it is so named will presently be apparent. It is nearly night when we leave St. Cloud for a four-mile ride to our quarters.

We can see in the rays of the setting sun, as

we ride over the prairie, our village of white tents pitched by the roadside, and our wagons parked near by. It is an exhilarating scene, bringing to remembrance the many tented fields during the war, and those soul-stirring days when the armies of the Republic marched under their great leader to victory.

The sun goes down through a blood-colored haze, throwing its departing beams upon a bank of leaden clouds that lie along the horizon. Old salts say that such sunsets in the tropics are followed by storms.

Through the evening, while sitting in the doors of our tents and talking of camp-life and its pleasant experiences, we can see faint flashes of lightning along the horizon. The leaden clouds grow darker, and rise slowly up the sky. Through the deepening haze we catch faint glimpses of celestial architecture, — castles, towers, massive walls, and

"Looming bastions fringed with fire."

Far away rolls the heavy thunder, — so far that it seems the diapason of a distant organ. We lose sight of the gorgeous palaces, temples, and cathedrals of the upper air, or we see them only when the bright flashes of lightning illume the sky.

It is past midnight, — we have been asleep, and are wakened by the sudden bursting of the storm. The canvas roof and walls of our house flap suddenly in the wind. The cords are drawn taut against the tent-pins. The roof rises, settles, surges up and down, to and fro, the walls belly in and then out against the swaying frame. The rain comes in great drops, in small drops, in drifting spray, rattling upon the canvas like a hundred thousand muskets, — just as they rattled and rolled on that awful day at the Wilderness when the two greatest armies ever gathered on this continent met in deadly conflict.

All the while the tent is as bright with lightning as with the sun at noonday. By the side of my cot is a book which I have been reading; taking it in my hand, I read the finest print, noted the hour, minute, and position of the second-hand upon my watch.

Looking out through the opening of the fly, I behold the distant woodland, the fences, the bearded grain laid prostrate by the blast, the rain-drops falling aslant through the air, the farm-house a half-mile distant, — all revealed by the red glare of the lightning. All the landscape is revealed. For an instant I am in darkness, then all appears again beneath the lurid light.

The storm grows wilder. The gale becomes a tempest, and increases to a tornado. The thunder crashes around, above, so near that the crackling follows in an instant the blinding flash. It rattles, rolls, roars, and explodes like bursting bombs.

The tent is reeling. Knowing what will be the

IN THE STORM.

result, I hurry on my clothing, and have just time to seize an india-rubber coat before the pins are pulled from the ground. I spring to the pole, determined to hold on to the last.

Though the lightning is so fearful, and the moment well calculated to arouse solemn thoughts, we cannot restrain our laughter when two occupants of an adjoining tent rush into mine in the condition of men who have had a sousing in a pond. The wind pulled their tent up by the roots, and slapped the wet canvas down upon them in a twinkling. They crawled out like muskrats from their holes, — their night-shirts fit for mops, their clothing ready for washing, their boots full of water, their hats limp and damp and ready for moulding into corrugated tiles.

It is a ludicrous scene. I am the central figure inside the tent, — holding to the pole with all my might, bareheaded, barefooted, my body at an angle of forty-five degrees, my feet sinking into the black mire, — the dripping canvas swinging and swaying, now lifted by the wind and now flapping in my face, and drenching anew two members of Congress, who sit upon my broken-down bed, shivering while wringing out their shirts!

When the fury of the storm is over, I rush out to drive down the pins, and find that my tent is the only one in the encampment that is not wholly prostrated. The members of the party are standing like *shirted* ghosts in the storm. The rotund form of our M. D. is wrapped in the oil-cloth table-cover. For the moment he is a hydropath, and complacently surveys the wreck of tents. The rain falls on his bare head, the water streams from his gray locks, and runs like a river down his broad back; but he does not bow before the blast, he breasts it bravely. I do not hear him, but I can see by his features that he is silently singing the Sunday-school song, —

"I 'll stand the storm,
It won't be long."

Tents, beds, bedding, clothing, all are soppy and moppy, and the ground a quagmire. We go ankle deep into the mud. We might navigate the prairies in a boat.

Our purveyor, Mr. Brackett, an old campaigner, knows just what to do to make us comfortable. He has a dry tent in one of the wagons, which, when the rain has ceased, is quickly set up. His cook soon has his coffee-pot bubbling, and with hot coffee and a roaring fire we are none the worse for the drenching.

The storm has spent its fury, and is passing away, but the heavens are all aglow. Broad flashes sweep across the sky, flame up to the zenith, or quiver along the horizon. Bolt after bolt falls earthward, or flies from the north, south, east, and west,—from all points of the compass,—branching into beautiful forms, spreading out into threads and fibres of light, each tipped with golden balls or beads of brightest hue, seen a moment, then gone forever.

Flash and flame, bolt and bar, bead, ball, and line, follow each other in quick succession, or all appear at once in indescribable beauty and fearful grandeur. We can only gaze in wonder and admiration, though all but blinded by the vivid flashes, and though each bolt may be a messenger of death,—though in the twinkling of an eye the spirit may be stricken from its present tabernacle and sent upon its returnless flight. The display, so magnificent and grand, has its only counterpart in the picture which imagination paints of Sinai or the final judgment.

In an adjoining county the storm was attended by a whirlwind. Houses were demolished and several persons killed. It was terrifying to be in it, to hear the deafening thunder; but it was a sight worth seeing,—that glorious lighting up of the arch of heaven.

It required half a day of bright sunshine to put things in trim after the tornado, and then on Saturday afternoon the party pushed on to Cold Spring and encamped on the bank of Sauk River for the Sabbath.

The camp was named "Jay Cooke," in honor of

the energetic banker who is the financial agent of the Northern Pacific Railroad Company. Sweet, calm, and peaceful the hours. Religious services were held, conducted by Rev. Dr. Lord, who had a flour-barrel and a candle-box before him for a pulpit; a congregation of teamsters, with people from the little village near by, and the gentlemen composing our party, some of us seated on boxes, but most of us sitting upon the ground. Nor were we without a choir. Everybody sung Old Hundred; and though some of us could only sound one note, and that straight along from beginning to end, like the drone of a bagpipe, it went gloriously. Old Hundred never was sung with better spirit, though there was room for improvement of the understanding, especially in the base. The teamsters, after service, hunted turtle-eggs on the bank of the river, and one of them brought in a hatful, which were cooked for supper.

Our course from Cold Spring was up the Sauk Valley to Sauk Centre, a lively town with an excellent water-power. The town is about six years old, but its population already numbers fifteen hundred. The country around it is one of the most beautiful and fertile imaginable. The Sauk River is the southern boundary of the timbered lands west of the Mississippi. As we look southward, over the magnificent expanse, we see farm-houses and grain-fields, but on the north bank are dense forests.

CAMP JAY COOKE.

The prairie lands are already taken up by settlers, while there are many thousand acres of the wooded portion of Stearns County yet in the possession of the government. The emigrant can raise a crop of wheat the second year after beginning a farm upon the prairies, while if he goes into the woods there is the slow process of clearing and digging out of stumps, and a great deal of hard labor before he has any returns. Those prairie lands that lie in the immediate vicinity of timber are most valuable. The valley of the Sauk, besides being exceedingly fertile, has timber near at hand, and has had a rapid development. It is an inviting section for the capitalist, trader, mechanic, or farmer, and its growth promises to be as rapid in the future as it has been since 1865.

A two days' ride over a magnificent prairie brings us to White Bear Lake. If we had travelled due west from St. Cloud, along the township lines, sixty miles, we should have found ourselves at its southern shore instead of its northern. Our camp for the night was pitched on the hills overlooking this sheet of water. The Vale of Tempe could not have been fairer, and Arcadia had no lovelier scene, than that which we gazed upon from the green slope around our tents, blooming with wild roses, lilies, petunias, and phlox.

The lake stretches southward a distance of twelve miles, indented here and there by a wooded promontory, with sandy beaches sweeping in magnificent curves, with a patch of woodland on the eastern shore, and a green fringe of stately oaks and elms around its entire circumference. As far as the vision extends we behold limitless fields, whose verdure changes in varying hues with every passing cloud, and wanting only a background of highlands to make it as lovely as Windermere, the most enchanting of all the lakes of Old England.

At our feet was the little town of Glenwood. We looked down upon a hotel with the stars and stripes waving above it; upon a neat school-house with children playing around its doors; upon a cluster of twenty or thirty white houses surrounded by gardens and flower-beds. Three years ago this was a solitude.

There is a sail-boat upon the lake, which some gentlemen of our party chartered for a fishing-excursion. Thinking perhaps we should get more fish by dividing our force, I took a skiff, and obtained a stalwart Norwegian to row it. Almost as soon as my hook touched the water I felt a tug at the other end of the line, and in came a pickerel, —a three-pounder! The Norwegian rowed slowly along the head of the lake, and one big fellow after another was pulled into the boat. There was scarcely a breath of wind, and the sails were idly flapping against the masts of the larger boat, where my friends were whiling away the time as best they could, tantalized by seeing that I was having all the fun. They could only crack their rifles at a loon, or at the flocks of ducks swimming along the shore.

But there was rare sport at hand. I discovered an enormous turtle lying upon the surface of the water as if asleep. "Approach gently," I said to the Norwegian. He dipped his oars softly, and sent the skiff stern foremost towards the turtle, who was puffing and blowing like a wheezy old gentleman sound asleep.

One more push of the oar and he will be mine. Too late! We have lost him. Down he goes. I can see him four feet beneath us, clawing off. No, he is coming up. He rises to the surface. I grasp his tail with both hands, and jerk with all my might. The boat dips, but a backward spring saves it from going over, and his majesty of White Bear Lake, the oldest inhabitant of its silver waters, weighing forty-six pounds,—so venerable that he wears a garden-bed of grass and weeds upon his back—is floundering in the half-filled skiff.

The boatman springs to his feet, stands on the seat with uplifted oar, undecided whether to jump overboard or to fight the monster who is making at his legs with open jaws.

By an adroit movement of an oar I whirl him upon his back, and hold him down while the Norwegian paddles slowly to the beach.

The captive rides in a meal-bag the remainder of the day, hissing now and then, and striving to regain his liberty.

Ah ! is n't that a delicious supper which we sit down to out upon the prairies on the shores of Lightning Lake, — beyond the borders of civilization ! It is not mock turtle, but the genuine article, such as aldermen eat. True, we have tin cups and plates, and other primitive table furniture, but hunger sharpens the appetite, and food is as toothsome as if served on gold-bordered china. Besides turtle-soup we have fresh fish and boiled duck. Who is there that would not like to find such fare inside the borders of civilization ?

Beyond Pope we entered Grant County, containing 268,000 acres of land, nearly all open to settlement, and through which the main line of the St. Paul and Pacific Railroad will be constructed the present year. The population of the entire county probably does not exceed five hundred, who are mostly Swedes and Norwegians. It is on the ridge, or, rather, the gentle undulating prairie, between the waters of the Red River of the North and the Chippewa River, an affluent of the Minnesota. We passed between two small lakes; the waters of one find their way to the Gulf of Mexico, the other to the Arctic Sea.

Our second Sabbath camp was upon the bank of the Red River of the North, — a beautiful stream, winding its peaceful way through a country as fertile as the Delta of the Nile.

For two days we had journeyed over rolling prairie, seeing no inhabitant; but on Saturday afternoon we reached the great thoroughfare leading from the Mississippi to the Red River, — travelled by the Fort Abercrombie stage, and by the Pembina and Fort Garry carts, by government trains and the ox-teams that transport the supplies of the Hudson Bay Company.

Sitting there upon the bank of the Red River amid the tall, rank grasses, and watching the flowing stream, my thoughts went with its tide towards the Northern Sea. It has its rise a hundred miles or more north of us, near Lake Itasca, the source of the Mississippi, flows southward to this point, turns westward here, is joined below by a stream issuing from Lake Traverse, its most southern source, and then flows due north to Lake Winnipeg, a distance altogether of about five hundred miles.

It is the great southern artery of a water-system that lies almost wholly beyond the jurisdiction of the United States.

The Assinniboine joins it just before reaching Lake Winnipeg, and up that stream we may steam due west two hundred and thirty miles to Fort Ellis. From Winnipeg we may pass eastward to the intricate Rainy Lake system towards Superior, or westward into Lakes Manitoba and Winnipegosis, which together contain as much water as Lake Erie.

Sailing along the western shore of Lake Winnipeg two hundred miles, we reach the mouth of the Saskatchawan, large enough to be classed as one of the great rivers of the continent.

Professor Hind, of Toronto, who conducted a government exploring-party through the country northwest of Lake Superior, says: "The Saskatchawan, which gathers the waters from a country greater in extent than the vast region drained by the St. Lawrence and all its tributaries, from Lake Superior to the Gulf, is navigable for more than a thousand miles of its course, with the single exception of a few rapids near its confluence with Lake Winnipeg."

Professor Hind travelled from Fort Garry northwest over the prairies towards the Rocky Mountains, and gives the following description of his first view of the stream. He says: —

"The first view, six hundred miles from the lake, filled me with astonishment and admiration, — nearly half a mile broad, flowing with a swift current, and still I was three hundred and fifty miles from the mountains."

The small steamer now plying on the Red River might, during the season of high water, make its way from Fort Abercrombie down this river, then through Lake Winnipeg, and up the Saskatchawan westward to the base of the Rocky Mountains, — a distance altogether of sixteen hundred miles.

We are in the latitude of the continental water-system. If we travel along the parallel eastward, one hundred miles will bring us to the Mississippi at Crow Wing, another hundred will take us to Lake Superior, where we may embark on a propeller of five hundred tons and make our way down through the lakes and the St. Lawrence to Liverpool, or any other foreign port; or travelling west three hundred miles will bring us to the Missouri, where we may take one of the steamers plying on that stream and go up to Fort Benton under the shadow of the Rocky Mountains.

Two hundred and fifty miles farther by land, through the mining region of Montana, will bring us to the navigable waters of the Columbia, down which we may glide to the Pacific.

Nowhere in the Eastern hemisphere is there such a succession of lakes and navigable rivers, and no other country exhibits such an area of arable land so intersected by fresh-water streams.

It would be an easy matter by canals to connect the Red River, the Saskatchawan, and Lake Winnipeg with the Mississippi. We can take a canoe from this point and paddle up to Otter-Tail Lake, and there, by carrying it a mile or so over a sand-ridge, launch it on Leaf River, an affluent of the Crow-Wing, and so reach the Father of Waters. We may do even better than that. Instead of paddling up stream we may float down with the current a few miles to the outlet of Lake Traverse, row across the lake, and from that into Big Stone Lake, which is the source of the Minnesota River, and by this route reach the Mississippi below Minneapolis. Boats carrying two tons have frequently passed from one river to the other during the season of high water. It would not be difficult to construct a canal by which steamers might pass from the Mississippi to the base of the Rocky Mountains in British Columbia. Railroads are superseding canals, and it is not likely that any such improvement of the water-way will be attempted during the present generation.

But a glance at the river and lake systems enables us to obtain a view of the physical features of the country. We see that the northwestern portion of the continent is an extended plain. The Red River here by our encampment is about nine hundred and sixty feet above the sea. If we were to float down to Lake Winnipeg, we should find that sheet of water three hundred feet lower.

Our camp is pitched to-day about ten miles west of the 96th meridian. If we were to travel south from this point 350 miles, we should reach Omaha, which is 946 feet above the sea, so that if we were sitting on the bank of the Missouri at that point, we should be just about as high above tide-water as we are while lolling here in the tall rank grass. By going from Omaha to San Francisco over the Pacific Railroad, we see the elevations of the country; then by striking westward from this point to the head-waters of the Missouri, and then down the Columbia, we shall see at once the physical features of the two sections. The engineers of the Pacific Railroad, after gaining the top of the bluff behind Omaha, have a long and apparently level sweep before them. Yet there is a gradually ascending grade. Four hundred and eighty-five miles west of Omaha we come to the 104th meridian, at an elevation of 4,861 feet. If we go west from this point to that meridian, we shall strike it at the mouth of the Yellowstone, 1,970 feet above tide-water. Near the 105th meridian is the highest point on the Union Pacific, at Sherman, which is 8,235 feet above the sea. Three hundred miles beyond Sherman, at Green River, is the lowest point between Omaha and the descent into Salt Lake Valley, 6,112 feet above the ocean level. At that point we are about twenty-six miles west of the 110th meridian. Now going northward to the valley of the Missouri once more, we find that Fort Benton is about the same number of miles west of the same meridian, but the fort is only 2,747 feet above the sea.

Just beyond Fort Benton we come to the Rocky

Mountains,—the only range to be crossed between Lake Superior and the Columbia. We enter the Deer Lodge Pass near the 112th meridian, where our barometer will show us that we are about five thousand feet above the sea. We find that the miners at work on the western slope have cut a canal through the pass, and have turned the waters of the Missouri into the Columbia. The pass is so level that the traveller can hardly tell when he has reached the dividing line.

Going south now along the meridian, we shall find that between Green River and Salt Lake lies the Wasatch Range, which the Union Pacific crosses at an elevation of 7,463 feet at Aspen Station, 940 miles west of Omaha. From that point the line descends to Salt Lake, which is 4,220 feet above the sea. Westward of this, on the 115th meridian, 1,240 miles from Omaha, we reach the top of Humboldt Mountains, 6,169 feet above tidewater, while the elevation is only 1,500 feet on the same meridian in the valley of the Columbia.

At Humboldt Lake, 1,493 miles west of Omaha, the rails are at the lowest level of the mountain region, 4,047 feet above the sea. This is a little west of the 119th meridian, about the same longitude as Walla Walla on the great plain of the Columbia, which is less than 400 feet above the sea.

Westward of Humboldt Lake the Central Line rises to the summit of the Sierra Nevadas, crossing them 7,042 feet above the sea, then descending at the rate of 116 feet to the mile into the valley of the Sacramento.

Now going back to the plains, to the town of Sidney, which is 410 miles west of Omaha, we find the altitude there the same as at Humboldt Lake. This level does not show itself again till we are well down on the western slope of the Sierra Nevada Range. The entire country between Omaha and Sacramento, with the exception of about 510 miles, is above the level of 4,000 feet, while on the line westward from the point where I am indulging in this topographical revery there are not thirty miles reaching that altitude.

With this glance at the configuration of the continent I might make an isometric map in the sand with my fingers, heaping it up to represent the Black Hills at Sherman, a lower ridge to indicate the Wasatch Range, a depression to show the Salt Lake Valley, and then another high ridge to represent the Sierra Nevadas. I might trace the channel of the Missouri and the Columbia, and show that most of this territory is a great plain sloping northward, — that it is lower at Winnipeg than it is here, as low here as it is at Omaha.

Taking this glance at the physical features of the northern and central portions of the continent, I can see that nature has adapted all this vast area drained by the Missouri and Yellowstone and

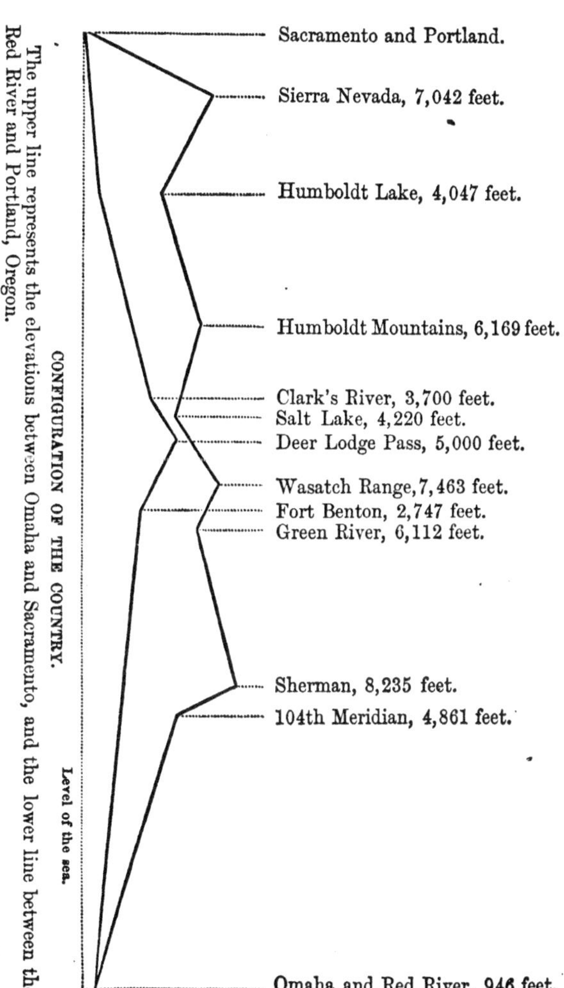

CONFIGURATION OF THE COUNTRY.

The upper line represents the elevations between Omaha and Sacramento, and the lower line between the Red River and Portland, Oregon.

their tributaries, by the Mississippi, by the Red River, the Assinniboine, the Saskatchawan, and the Columbia, to be the abode, in the future, of uncounted millions of the human race.

It is a solitude now, but the vanguard of the approaching multitude is near at hand. The farmer who lives up the stream and tends the ferry where we crossed yesterday has one neighbor within twelve miles; but a twelvemonth hence these acres will have many farm-houses. To-day we have listened to a sermon by the Rev. Dr. Lord, who preached beneath a canvas roof. We were called together by the blowing of a tin trumpet, but a year hence the sweet and solemn tones of church-bells will in all probability echo over these verdant meadows.

The locomotive — that great civilizer of this century — will be here before the flowers bloom in the spring of 1871. It will bring towns, villages, churches, school-houses, printing-presses, and millions of free people. I sit as in a dream. I can hear, in imagination, the voices of the advancing multitude, — of light-hearted maidens and sober matrons, of bright-eyed boys and strong-armed men. The wild roses are blooming here to-day, the sod is as yet unturned, and the lilies of the field hold up their cups to catch the falling dew; but another year will bring the beginning of the change. Civilization, which has crossed the Mississippi, will soon flow down this stream, and sweep on to the valley of the Upper Missouri.

Think of it, young men of the East, you who are measuring off tape for young ladies through the long and wearisome hours, barely earning your living! Throw down the yardstick and come out here if you would be men. Let the fresh breeze fan your brow, take hold of the plough, bend down for a few years to hard work with determination to win nobility, and success will attend your efforts. Is this too enthusiastic? Will those who read it say, "He has lost his head and gone daft out there on the prairies"? Not quite. I am an observer here, as I have been in other lands. I have ridden many times over the great States of the Northwest; have seen the riches of Santa Clara and Napa west of the Sierra Nevadas; have looked out over the meadows of the Yangtse and the Nile, and can say, with honest conviction, that I have seen nowhere so inviting a field as that of Minnesota, none with greater undeveloped wealth, or with such prospect of quick development.

CHAPTER III.

THE RED RIVER COUNTRY.

MONDAY morning saw us on our way northward, — down the valley of the Red River. It was exhilarating to gallop over the level prairies, inhaling the fresh air, our horses brushing the dew from the grass, and to see flocks of plump prairie chickens rise in the air and whirr away, — to mark where they settled, and then to start them again and bring them down, one by one, with a double-barrelled shot-gun. Did we not think of the stews and roasts we would have at night?

For a dozen years or more every school-boy has seen upon his map the town of Breckenbridge, located on the Red River of the North. It is off from the travelled road. The town, as one of our teamsters informed us, "has gone up." It originally consisted of two houses and a saw-mill, but the Sioux Indians swooped down upon it in 1862, and burned the whole place. A few logs, the charred remains of timbers, and tall fire-weeds alone mark the spot.

Riding on, we reached Fort Abercrombie at noon. It is situated in Dakota, on the west bank of the Red River, which we crossed by a rope ferry. It is a resting-place for the thousands of teams passing between St. Cloud and Fort Garry, and other places in the far Northwest. The place is of no particular account except as a distributing point for government supplies for forts farther on, and the advancement of civilization will soon enable the War Department to break up the establishment.

The river is fringed with timber. We ride beneath stately oaks growing upon the bottom-lands, and notice upon the trees the high-water marks of former years. The stream is very winding, and when the spring rains come on the rise is as great, though not usually so rapid, as in the Merrimac and Connecticut, and other rivers of the East.

The valley of the Red River is not such as we are accustomed to see in the East, bounded by hills or mountains, but a level plain.

When the sky is clear and the air serene, we can catch far away in the east the faint outline of the Leaf Hills, composing the low ridge between the Red River and the Mississippi, but westward there is nothing to bound the sight. The dead level reaches on and on to the rolling prairies of the Upper Missouri.

The eye rests only upon the magnificent carpet, bright with wild roses and petunias, lilies and harebells, which Nature has unrolled upon the floor of this gorgeous palace.

I had been slow to believe all that had been told in regard to the genial climate of the Northwest, but through the courtesy of the commandant of the Fort, General Hunt, was permitted to see the meteorological records kept at the post.

The summer of 1868 was excessively warm in the Western, Middle, and Atlantic States. Here, on one day in July, the mercury rose to ninety degrees, Fahrenheit, but the mean temperature for the month was seventy-nine. In August the highest temperature was eighty-eight, the lowest fifty, the mean sixty-nine. In September the highest temperature was seventy-four, the mean forty-seven. A slight frost occurred on the night of the 16th, and a hard one on the last day of the month. In October a few flakes of snow fell on the 27th. In November there were a few inches of snow. Toward the close of December, on one day, the mercury reached twenty-seven below zero. On the 30th of January it dropped to thirty below. During this month there were four days on which snow fell, and in February there were ten snowy days. The greatest depth of snow during the winter was about eighteen inches, furnishing uninterrupted sleighing from December to March.

On the 23d of March wild geese and ducks appeared, winging their way to Lake Winnipeg and Hudson Bay. The spring opened early in April.

There are no farms as yet in the valley, — the few settlers cultivating only small patches of land.

I have thought of this section of country as being almost up to the arctic circle, and can only disabuse my mind by comparing it with other localities in the same latitude. St. Paul is in the latitude of Bordeaux, in the grape-growing district of Southern France. Here at Fort Abercrombie we are at least one hundred and fifty miles farther south than the world's gayest capital, Paris.

It is not likely that Northern Minnesota will ever become a wine-producing country, though wild grapes are found along the streams, and the people of St. Paul and Minneapolis will show us thrifty vines in their gardens, laden with heavy clusters.

Minnesota is a wheat-growing region, climate and soil are alike favorable to its production.

On the east bank of the Red River we see a field owned by Mr. McAuley, who keeps a store and sells boots, pipes, tobacco, powder, shot, and all kinds of supplies needed by hunters and frontiersmen. He sowed his wheat this year (1869) on the 5th of May, and it is now, on the 19th of July, heading out. "I had forty-five bushels to the acre last year," he says, "and the present crop will be equally good."

This Red River Valley throughout its length and breadth is very fertile. Here are twenty thousand square miles of land, — an area as large as

Vermont and New Hampshire combined, — unsurpassed for richness.

The construction of the Northern Pacific Railroad and the St. Paul and Pacific, both of which are to reach this valley within a few months, will make these lands virtually as near market as the farms of Central or Western Illinois. From the Red River to Duluth the distance is 210 miles in a direct line. It is 187 miles from Chicago to Springfield, Illinois; so that when the Northern Pacific Railroad is constructed to this point, Mr. McAuley will be just as near Boston or New York as the farmers who live in the vicinity of the capital of Illinois; for grain can be taken from Duluth to Buffalo, Oswego, or Ogdensburg as cheaply as from Chicago. The richness of the lands, the supply of timber on the Red River and all its branches, with the opening of the two lines of railway, will give a rapid settlement to this paradise of the Northwest.

Professor Hind, of Toronto, who was sent out by the Canadian government to explore the British Possessions northwest of Lake Superior, in his report says: "Of the valley of the Red River I find it impossible to speak in any other terms than those which may express astonishment and admiration. I entirely concur in the brief but expressive description given me by an English settler on the Assinniboine, that the valley of the Red River, including a large portion belonging to its great affluents, is a paradise of fertility."

In Mr. McAuley's garden we see corn in the spindle. The broad leaves wear as rich a green as if fertilized with the best Peruvian guano; and no wonder, for the soil is a deep black loam, and as mellow as an ash-heap. His peas were sown the 2d of June, and they are already large enough for the table! He will have an abundant supply of cucumbers by the first of August. They were not started under glass, but the dry seeds were dropped in the hills the same day he planted his peas, — the 2d of June.

Vegetation advances with great rapidity. Mr. McAuley says that vegetables and grains come to maturity ten or fifteen days earlier here than at Manchester, New Hampshire, where he once resided.

General Pope was formerly stationed at Fort Abercrombie; and in his report upon the resources of the country and its climatology, says that the wheat, upon an average, is five pounds per bushel heavier than that grown in Illinois or the Middle States.

We saw yesterday a gentleman and lady who live at Fort Garry, and who call themselves "Winnipeggers." They were born in Scotland, and had been home to Old Scotia to see their friends.

"How do you like Winnipeg?" I asked.

"There is no finer country in the world," he replied.

"Do you not have cold winters?"

"Not remarkably so. We have a few cold days, but the air is usually clear and still on such days, and we do not mind the cold. If we only had a railroad, it would be the finest place in the world to live in."

We wonder at his enthusiasm over a country which we have thought of as being almost, if not quite, out of the world, while he doubtless looks with pity upon us who are content to remain in such a cooped-up place as the East.

Most of us, unless we have become nomads, think that there are no garden patches so attractive as our own, and we wonder how other people can be willing to live so far off.

This Winnipeg gentleman says that the winters are no more severe at Fort Garry than at St. Paul, and that the spring opens quite as early.

The temperature for the year at Fort Garry is much like that of Montreal, as will be seen by the following comparison: —

	Spring.	Summer.	Autumn.	Winter.
Montreal,	43°	70°	49°	17°
Fort Garry,	36	68	48	7

This shows the mean temperatures for the three months of each season. Though the mercury is ten degrees lower at Fort Garry in the winter than at Montreal, there is less wind, fewer raw days, much less snow, and, taken all in all, the climate is more agreeable.

Bidding good by to the courteous commander of the fort, who supplies that portion of our party going to the Missouri with an escort, we gallop on through this "Paradise," starting flocks of plovers from the waving grass, and bringing down, now and then, a prairie chicken.

Far away, on the verge of the horizon, we can see our wagons, — mere specks.

What a place for building a railway! Not a hillock nor a hollow, not a curve or loss of gradient; timber enough on the river for ties. And when built, what a place to let on steam! The engineer may draw his throttle-valve and give the piston full head. Here will be the place to see what iron, steel, and steam can do.

We pitch our tents for the night in the suburbs of Burlington, not far from the hotel and post-office. The hotel, which just now is the only building in town, is built of logs. It is not very spacious inside, but it has all the universe outside!

Once a week the mail-carrier passes from Fort Abercrombie to Pembina, and as there are a half-

RED RIVER VALLEY

dozen pioneers and half-breeds within a radius of thirty miles of Burlington, a post-office has been established here, which is kept in a shed adjoining the hotel.

The postmaster gives us a cordial greeting. It is a pleasure to hear this bluff but wide-awake German say, "O, I have been acquainted with you for a long while. I followed you through the war and around the world."

From first to last, in letters from the battle-field, from the various countries of the world, and in these notes of travel, it has ever been my aim to write for the comprehension of the people; and such spontaneous and uncalled-for commendation of my efforts out here upon the prairies was more grateful than many a well-meant paragraph from the public press.

While pitching our tents, a flock of pigeons flew past, and down in the woods along the bank of the river we could hear their cooing. Those who had shot-guns went to the hunt; while some of us tried the river for fish, but returned luckless. The supper was good enough, however, without trout or pickerel. Who can ask for anything better than prairie chicken, plover, duck, pork, and pigeons?

Then, when hunger is appeased, we sit around the camp-fire and think of the future of this paradise. Near by is another camp-fire.

I see by its glimmering light a stalwart man with shaggy beard and a slouched hat. The emigrant's wife sits on the other side of the fire, and by its light I see that she wears a faded linsey-woolsey dress, that her hair is uncombed, and that she has not given much attention to her toilet. Two frowzy-headed children, a boy and a girl, are romping in the grass. The worldly effects of this family are in that canvas-covered ox-wagon, with a chicken-coop at the hinder part, and a tin kettle dangling beneath the axle. This emigrant has come from Iowa. He is moving into this valley "to take up a claim." That is, he is going to select a piece of choice land under the Homestead Act, build a cabin, and "make a break in the per-ra-ry," he says.

He will be followed by others. The tide is setting in rapidly, and by the time the railway company are ready to carry freight there will be population enough here to support the road.

We have an early start in the morning. Our route is along a highway, upon which there is more travel than upon many of the old turnpikes of New England for Winnipeg, and the Hudson Bay posts receive all their supplies over this road.

At our noonday halt we fall in with Father Genin, a French Catholic priest, who lives on the bank of the river in a log-hut. He comes out to see us, wearing a long black bombazine priestly gown, and low-crowned hat. He is in the prime of life, was educated at Paris, came to Quebec, and is assigned to the Northwest. He has sailed over Lake Winnipeg, and paddled his canoe on the Saskatchawan and Athabasca.

"My parish," he says, "reaches from St. Paul to the Rocky Mountains." He speaks in glowing terms of the country up "in the Northwest," — as if we, who are now sixteen hundred miles from Boston, had not reached the Northwest!

Our talk with Father Genin, and his enthusiastic description of the Saskatchawan Valley, has set us to thinking of this region, to which the United States once held claim, and which might now have been a part of our domain if it had not been for the pusillanimity of President Polk.

Mackenzie was the first European who gave to the world an account of the country lying between us and the Arctic Sea. He was in this valley in 1789, and was charmed with it. He made his way down to Lake Winnipeg, thence up the Saskatchawan to Athabasca Lake. At the carrying-place between the Saskatchawan and Athabasca rivers, at Portage la Loche, he discovered springs of petroleum, which are thus described: —

"Twenty-five miles from the fork are some bituminous springs, into which a pole may be inserted without the least resistance. The bitumen is in a fluid state, and when mixed with resin is used to gum the canoes. In its heated state it emits a smell like sea-coal. The banks of Slave River, which are elevated, discover veins of the same bituminous quality." *

His winter quarters were near Lake Athabasca, at Fort Chippewayan, more than thirteen hundred miles northwest from Chicago. He thus writes in regard to the country: —

"In the fall of 1787, when I first arrived at Athabasca, Mr. Pond was settled on the bank of the Elk River, where he remained three years, and had as fine a kitchen-garden as I ever saw in Canada" (p. 127).

Of the climate in winter he says that the beginning was cold, and about one foot of snow fell. The last week in December and the first week in January were marked by warm southwest breezes, which dissolved all the snow. Wild geese appeared on the 13th of March; and on the 5th of April the snow had entirely disappeared. On the 20th he wrote: —

"The trees are budding, and many plants are in blossom" (p. 150).

Mackenzie left the "Old Establishment," as one of the posts of the Hudson Bay Company was called, on the Peace River, in the month of May, for the Rocky Mountains. He followed the stream through the gap of the mountains, passed to the

* General History of the Fur-Trade, p. 87.

head-waters of Fraser River, and descended that stream to the Pacific. He thus describes the country along the Peace River: —

"This magnificent theatre of nature has all the decorations which the trees and animals can afford it. Groves of poplars in every shape vary the scene, and their intervales are relieved with vast herds of elk and buffaloes, — the former choosing the steeps and uplands, the latter preferring the plains. The whole country displayed an exuberant verdure; the trees that bear blossoms were advancing fast to that delightful appearance, and the velvet rind of their branches reflecting the oblique rays of a rising or setting sun added a splendid gayety to the scene which no expressions of mine are qualified to describe" (p. 154).

This was in latitude 55° 17′, about fourteen hundred miles from St. Paul.

The next traveller who enlightened the world upon this region was Mr. Harman, a native of Vergennes, Vermont, who became connected with the Northwest Fur Company, and passed seventeen years in British America. He reached Lake Winnipeg in 1800, and his first winter was passed west of the lake. Under date of January 5th we have this record in his journal: —

"Beautiful weather. Saw in different herds at least a thousand buffaloes grazing" (p. 68).

"*February* 17*th.* — We have now about a foot

and a half of snow on the ground. This morning one of our people killed a buffalo on the prairie opposite the fort" (p. 73).

"*March* 14*th*. — The greater part of the snow is dissolved." *

On the 6th of April Mr. Harman writes: "I have taken a ride on horseback to a place where our people are making sugar. My path led me over a small prairie, and through a wood, where I saw a great variety of birds that were straining their tuneful throats as if to welcome the return of another spring; small animals were running about, or skipping from tree to tree, and at the same time were to be seen, swans, bustards, ducks, etc. swimming about in the rivers and ponds. All these things together rendered my ramble beautiful beyond description" (p. 75).

During the month of April there were two snow-storms, but the snow disappeared nearly as fast as it fell.

One winter was passed by Mr. Harman in the country beyond Lake Athabasca, on the Athabasca River, where he says the snow during the winter "was at no time more than two feet and a half deep" (p. 174).

* On the 16th of March, 1870, while these notes were under review, the streets of Boston were deep with snow, and twenty-four trains were blockaded on the Boston and Albany Railroad between Springfield and Albany.

On May 6th he writes: "We have planted our potatoes and sowed most of our garden-seeds" (p. 178).

"*June 2d.* — The seeds which we sowed in the garden have sprung up and grown remarkably well. The present prospect is that strawberries, red raspberries, shad-berries, cherries, etc. will be abundant this season."

"*July 21st.* — We have cut down our barley, and I think it is the finest that I ever saw in any country. The soil on the points of land along this river is excellent" (p. 181).

"*October 3d.* — We have taken our potatoes out of the ground, and find that nine bushels which we planted on the 10th of May last have produced a little more than one hundred and fifty bushels. The other vegetables in our garden have yielded an increase much in the same proportion, which is sufficient proof that the soil of the points of land along this river is good. Indeed, I am of opinion that wheat, rye, barley, oats, peas, etc. would grow well in the plains around us" (p. 186).

He passed several winters at the head-waters of Peace River, in the Rocky Mountains. In his journal we have these records: —

"*May 7th.* — The weather is very fine, and vegetation is far advanced for the season. Swans and ducks are numerous in the lakes and rivers."

"*May 22d.* — Planted potatoes and sowed garden-seeds."

"*October 3d.* — We have taken our vegetables out of the ground. We have forty-one bushels of potatoes, the produce of one bushel planted last spring. Our turnips, barley, etc. have produced well" (p. 257).

In 1814 he writes under date of September 3d: "A few days since we cut down our barley. The five quarts which I sowed on the 1st of May have yielded as many bushels. One acre of ground, producing in the same proportion, would yield eighty-four bushels. This is sufficient proof that the soil in many places in this quarter is favorable to agriculture" (p. 267).

Sir John Richardson, who explored the arctic regions by this route, says: "Wheat is raised with profit at Fort Liard, lat. 60° 5′ N., lon. 122° 31′ W., and four or five hundred feet above the sea. This locality, however, being in the vicinity of the Rocky Mountains, is subject to summer frosts, and the grain does not ripen every year, though in favorable seasons it gives a good return."

In 1857, Captain Palliser, of the Royal Engineers, was sent out by the English government to explore the region between Lake Superior and the Pacific, looking towards the construction of a railroad across the continent, through the British Possessions. His report to the government is published in the Blue-Book.

Speaking of the country along the Assinniboine,

he says: "The Assinniboine has a course of nearly three hundred miles; lies wholly within a fertile and partially wooded country. The lower part of the valley for seventy miles, before it joins the Red River, affords land of surpassing richness and fertility" (p. 9).

Of the South Saskatchawan, he says that "it flows through a thick-wooded country" (p. 10).

The natural features of the north branch of that river are set forth in glowing language: —

"The richness of the natural pasture in many places on the North Saskatchawan and its tributary, Battle River, can hardly be exaggerated. Its value does not consist in its long rank grasses or in its great quantity, but from its fine quality, comprising nutritious species of grasses, along with natural vetches in great variety, which remain throughout the winter juicy and fit for the nourishment of stock.

"Almost anywhere along the Saskatchawan a sufficiency of good soil is everywhere to be found, fit for all purposes, both for pasture and tillage, extending towards the thick-wooded hills, and also to be found in the region of the lakes, between Forts Pitt and Edmonton. In almost every direction around Edmonton the land is fine, excepting only the hilly country at the higher level, such as the Beacon Hills; even there there is nothing like sterility, only the surface is too much broken to be occupied while more level country can be obtained" (p. 10).

Going up the Saskatchawan he discovered beds of coal, which are thus described: —

"In the upper part of the Saskatchawan country, coal of fine quality occurs abundantly, and may hereafter be very useful. It is quite fit to be employed in the smelting of iron from the ore of that metal, which occurs in large quantities in the same strata" (p. 11).

Two hundred miles north of this coal deposit, Mackenzie discovered the springs of petroleum and coal strata along the banks of the streams. Harman saw the same.

Palliser wintered on the Saskatchawan, and speaks thus of the climate: —

"The climate in winter is more rigorous than that of Red River, and partial thaws occur long before the actual opening of spring. The winter is much the same in duration, but the amount of snow that falls rapidly decreases as we approach the mountains. The river generally freezes about the 12th of November, and breaks up from the 17th to the 20th of April. During the winter season of five months the means of travelling and transport are greatly facilitated by the snow, the ordinary depth of which is sufficient for the use of sleighs, without at the same time being great enough to impede horses.

"The whole of this region of country would be valuable, not only for agriculture, but also for mixed purposes of settlement. The whole region is well wooded and watered, and enjoys a climate far preferable to that of either Sweden or Norway. I have not only seen excellent wheat, but Indian corn (which will not succeed in England or Ireland), ripening on Mr. Pratt's farm at the Qui Appelle Lakes in 1857" (p. 11).

Father De Smet, a Catholic missionary, in 1845 crossed the Rocky Mountains from British Columbia, eastward to the head-waters of the south branch of the Saskatchawan, and passed along the eastern base of the mountains to Edmonton. He characterizes the country as "an ocean of prairies."

"The entire region," he says, "in the vicinity of the eastern chain of the Rocky Mountains, serving as their base for thirty or sixty miles, is extremely fertile, abounding in forests, plains, prairies, lakes, streams, and mineral springs. The rivers and streams are innumerable, and on every side offer situations favorable for the construction of mills. The northern and southern branches of the Saskatchawan water the district I have traversed for a distance of about three hundred miles. Forests of pines, cypress, cedars, poplar and aspen trees, as well as others of different kinds, occupy a large portion of it. The country would be capable of supporting a large population, and the soil is favorable for the production of wheat, barley, potatoes, and beans, which grow here as well as in the more southern countries."

It is a region abundantly supplied with coal of the lignite formation. Father Genin has a specimen of lignite taken from the banks of Maple River, about seven miles from our camp. It is a small branch of the Red River flowing from the west. If we were to travel northwest a little more than one hundred miles, we should come to the Little Souris or Mouse River, a branch of the Assinniboine, where we should find seams of the same kind of coal. Continuing on to the Saskatchawan, we shall find it appearing all along the river from Fort Edmonton to the Rocky Mountains, a distance of between three and four hundred miles.

Dr. Hector, geologist to the exploring expedition under Captain Palliser, thus describes the coal on Red Deer River, a branch of the South Saskatchawan: —

"The lignite forms beds of great thickness, one group of seams measuring twenty-five feet in thickness, of which twelve feet consist of pure compact lignite. At one point the seam was on fire, and the Indians say that for as long as they can remember the fire at this place has not been extinguished, summer or winter" (p. 233).

Father De Smet passed down the river in 1845, and it was then on fire. If we were to travel northward from the Red Deer to the Peace River, we should find the same formation; and if we were to glide down the Mackenzie towards the Arctic Sea, we should, according to the intrepid voyager whose name it bears, find seams of coal along its banks.

Mr. Bourgeau, botanist to the Palliser Exploring Expedition, in a letter addressed to Sir William Hooker, has the following remarks upon the capabilities of the Northwest for supporting a dense population :—

"It remains for me to call the attention of the English government to the advantages there would be in establishing agricultural districts in the vast plains of Rupert's Land, and particularly in the Saskatchawan, in the neighborhood of Fort Carlton. This district is much better adapted to the culture of staple crops than one would have been inclined to believe from this high latitude. In effect, the few attempts at the culture of cereals already made in the vicinity of the Hudson Bay Company's posts demonstrate by their success how easy it would be to obtain products sufficiently large to remunerate the efforts of the agriculturist. Then, in order to put the land under cultivation, it would be necessary only to till the better portions of the soil. The prairies offer natural pasturage as favorable for the maintenance of numerous herds as if they had been artificially created. The construction of houses for habitation and for pioneer development would involve but little expense, because in many parts of the country, independent of wood, one would find fitting stones for building purposes, and it is easy to find clay for bricks. . . . . The vetches found here are as fitting for nourishment of cattle as the clover of European pasturage. The abundance of buffaloes, and the facility with which herds of horses and oxen increase, demonstrate that it would be enough to shelter animals in winter, and to feed them in the shelters with hay. . . . . In the gardens of the Hudson Bay Company's posts, beans, peas, and French beans have been successfully cultivated; also cabbages, turnips, carrots, rhubarb, and currants" (p. 250).

The winters of the Northwest are wholly unlike those of the Eastern and Middle States. The meteorologist of Palliser's Expedition says: "Along the eastern base of the Rocky Mountains there is a narrow strip of country in which there is never more than a few inches of snow on the ground. About forty miles to the eastward, however, the fall begins to be much greater, but during the winter rarely exceeds two feet. On the prairies the snow evaporates rapidly, and, except in hollows where it is drifted, never accumulates; but in the woods it is protected, and in spring is often from three to four feet deep" (p. 268).

Captain Palliser and party travelled from post to post during the winter without difficulty. In February, 1859, he travelled from Edmonton to Lake St. Ann's. On two nights the mercury was frozen in the bulb, — as it is not unfrequently at Franconia, New Hampshire. Exclusive of those two cold nights, the mean of the temperature was seventeen. He says: "This was a trip made during the coldest weather experienced in the country. If proper precautions are taken, there is nothing merely in extreme cold to stop travelling in the wooded country, but the danger of freezing from exposure upon the open plains is so great that they cannot be ventured on with safety during any part of the winter" (p. 268).

The Wesleyan Missionary Society of England has a mission at Edmonton, under the care of Rev. Thomas Woolsey. The following extracts from his journal will show the progress of the winter and spring season in 1855: —

"Nov. 1. A little snow has fallen for the first time.
" 12. Swamps frozen over.
" 13. A little more snow.
" 17. Crossed river on the ice.
Dec. 2. The past week has been remarkably mild.
" 9. More snow.
1856. Jan. 8 to 11. More like spring than winter.
Jan. 13. Fine open weather.
" 17. Somewhat colder.

Feb. 14. Weather open.
" 16. Snow rapidly disappearing.
Mar. 11. More snow.
" 17. Firing pasture-grounds to-day.
" 18. Thunder-storm.
" 21. Ducks and geese returning.
" 30. More snow, but it is rapidly disappearing.
" 31. Snow quite gone.
April 7. Ploughing commenced.
" 28. First wheat sown."

The succeeding winter was more severe, and three feet of snow fell during the season, but the spring opened quite as early as in 1856. The comparative mildness of the winter climate of all this vast area of the West and Northwest, at the head-waters of the Missouri, and in the British dominions, as far north as latitude 70°, is in a great measure due to the warm winds of the Pacific.

In the autumn of 1868 I crossed the Pacific, from Japan to San Francisco, in the Pacific mail-steamer Colorado. Soon after leaving the Bay of Yokohama we entered the Kuro-Siwo, or the Black Ocean River of the Asiatic coast. This ocean current bears a remarkable resemblance to the Gulf Stream of the Atlantic. Along the eastern shore of Japan the water, like that along Virginia and the Carolinas, is very cold, but we suddenly pass into the heated river, which, starting from the vicinity of the Philippine Islands, laves the eastern shore of Formosa, and rushes past the Bay of Yeddo at the rate of eighty miles per day. This heated river strikes across the Northern Pacific to British Columbia and Puget Sound, giving a genial climate nearly up to the Arctic Circle. No icebergs are ever encountered in the North Pacific. The influence of the Kuro-Siwo upon the Northwest is very much like that which the Gulf Stream has upon England and Norway. It gives to Oregon, Washington, British Columbia, and Vancouver Island winters so mild that the people cannot lay in a supply of ice for the summer. Roses bloom in the gardens throughout the year. So the water heated beneath the tropics, off the eastern coast of Siam and north of Borneo, flows along the shore of Japan up to the Aleutian Isles, imparting its heat to the air, which, under the universal law, ascends when heated, and sweeps over the Rocky Mountains, and tempers the climate east of them almost to Hudson Bay.

So wonderfully arranged is this mighty machinery of nature, that millions of the human race in coming years will rear their habitations and enjoy the blessings of civilization in regions that otherwise would be pathless solitudes.

In the meteorological register kept at Carlton House, in lat. 52° 51′, on the eastern limit of the Saskatchawan Plain, eleven hundred feet above the sea, we find this entry: "At this place westerly winds bring mild weather, and the easterly ones are attended by fog and snow."

By the following tabular statement we see at a glance the snow-fall at various places in the United States. We give average depths for the winter as set down in Blodget's climatology.

Oxford County, Maine	90	inches.
Dover, New Hampshire	68	"
Montreal, Canada	66	"
Burlington, Vermont	85	"
Worcester, Massachusetts	55	"
Cincinnati, Ohio	19	"
Burlington, Iowa	15	"
Beloit, Wisconsin	25	"
Fort Abercrombie, Dakota	12	"

From this testimony I am impelled to believe that the immense area west of Lake Superior and south of the 60th parallel is as capable of being settled as those portions of Russia, Sweden, and Norway south of that degree, now swarming with people. That parallel passes through St. Petersburg, Stockholm, Christiania, and the Shetland Isles on the eastern hemisphere, Fort Liard and Central Alaska on the western.

CHAPTER IV.

THE EMPIRE OF THE NORTHWEST.

HUNDREDS of Winnipeggers were upon the road, either going to or returning from St. Cloud, from whence all groceries and other supplies are obtained. The teams consist of a single horse or ox, not unfrequently a cow, harnessed to a two-wheeled cart. The outfit is a curiosity. The wheels are six or seven feet in diameter, and very dishing. A small rack is affixed to the wooden axle. The concern is composed wholly of wood, with a few raw-hide thongs. It is primitive in design and construction, and though so rude, though there is not an ounce of iron about the cart, it serves the purpose of these voyagers admirably. Our teams have been stuck in the mud, at the crossings of creeks, half a dozen times a day; but those high-wheeled carts are borne up by the grass roots where ours go down to the hub.

There is a family to each cart, — father, mother, and a troop of frowzy-headed, brown-faced children, who, though shoeless and hatless and half naked, are as happy as the larks singing in the meadows, or the plover skimming the air on quivering wings. They travel in companies, — fifteen or twenty carts in a caravan. When night comes on, the animals are turned out to graze; the families cook each their own scanty supply of food, smoke their pipes by the glimmering camp-fire, tell their stories of adventure among the buffaloes, roll themselves in a blanket, creep beneath their carts, — all the family in a pile if the night is cool, — sleep soundly, and are astir before daylight, and on the move by sunrise. The journey down and back is between eight and nine hundred miles; and as the average distance travelled is only about twenty miles a day, it takes from forty to fifty days to make the round trip. No wonder the people of that settlement are anxious to have a railroad reach the Red River.

Leaving the Pembina road and striking westward to the river, we descend the bank to the bottom-land, which is usually about twenty-five feet below the general surface of the valley. We cross the river by a rope ferry kept by a half-breed, and strike out upon the Dakota plain. The trail that we are upon bears northwest, and is the main road to Fort Totten, near Lake Miniwakan, or the "Devil's Lake," and the forts on the Upper Missouri. Here, as upon the Minnesota side, the wild-flowers are blooming in luxuriance. Our horses remorselessly trample the roses, the convolvulus, and the lilies beneath their feet.

The prairie chickens are whirring in every direction, and one of our bluff and burly teamsters, who is at home upon the prairies, who in the First Minnesota Regiment faced the Rebels in all the battles of the Peninsula, who was in the thickest of the fight at Gettysburg, who has hunted Indians over the Upper Missouri region, who is as keen-sighted as a hawk, takes the grouse right and left as they rise. His slouched hat bobs up and down everywhere. He seems to know just where the game is; now he is at your right hand, now upon the run a half-mile away upon the prairies. He stops, raises his gun, — there is a puff of smoke, another, and he has two more chickens in his bag. We are sure of having good suppers as long as he is about.

We reach Dakota City, — another thriving town of one log-house, — peopled by Monsieur Marchaud, a French Canadian, his Chippewa wife and twelve children.

While our tents are being pitched, we cross the river by another ferry to Georgetown, — a place consisting of two dwellings and a large storehouse owned by the Hudson Bay Company. This is the present steamboat landing, though sometimes the one steamer now on the river goes up to Fort Abercrombie. The river is narrow and winding south of this point, and not well adapted to navigation.

We find an obliging young Scotchman with a

thin-faced wife in possession of the property belonging to the Company. He takes care of the premises through the year on a salary of two hundred dollars, and has his tea, sugar, and groceries furnished him. He can cultivate as much land as he pleases, though he does not own a foot of it, — neither does the Company own an acre. It belongs to the people of the United States, and any brave young man with a large-hearted wife may become possessor of these beautiful acres if he will, with the moral certainty of finding them quadrupled in value in five years.

This great highway of the North lies along the eastern bank of the river. We have travelled over it all the way from Fort Abercrombie, passing and meeting teams. Here we see a train of thirty wagons drawn by oxen, loaded with goods consisting of boxes of tea, sugar, salt, pork, bacon, and bales of cloth, which are shipped by steamer from this landing. The teas come from England to Montreal, are there shipped to Milwaukie, and transported by rail to St. Cloud. Each chest is closely packed in canvas and taken through in bond. The transportation of the Hudson Bay Company between this place and St. Cloud amounts to about seven hundred tons per annum.

In addition, the Red River transportation carried on by the Indians and half-breeds is very large. About twenty-five hundred carts pass down and up this highway during the year, each one carrying upon an average nine hundred pounds.

Besides all this there is the United States government transportation to Fort Abercrombie and the forts beyond, amounting last year to eighteen hundred tons. The rates paid by the War Department government for transportation are $\$1.36\frac{3}{8}$ per hundred pounds for every hundred miles. All of this traffic will be transferred at once to the Northern Pacific Railroad upon its completion to the Red River.

The estimated value of the Red River trade is ten millions of dollars per annum, and it is increasing every year.

The keen-eyed hunters of our party have been on the lookout for a stray buffalo or a deer, but the buffaloes are a hundred miles away. We hear that they have come north of the Missouri in great numbers, and those who are to go West anticipate rare sport. For want of a buffalo-steak we put up with beef. It is juicy and tender, from one of Mr. Marchaud's heifers, which has been purchased for the party.

It is a supper fit for sovereigns, — and every one is a sovereign out here, on the unsurveyed lands, of which we, in common with the rest of the people, are proprietors. We are lords of the manor, and we have sat down to a feast. Our eggs are newly laid by the hens of Dakota City, our milk is fresh from the cows whose bells are tinkling in the bushes along the bank of the river, and the cakes upon our table are of the finest flour in the world. Hunger furnishes the best relish, and when the cloth is removed we sit around the camp-fire during the evening, passing away the hours with wit, repartee, and jest, mingled with sober argument and high intellectual thought.

Our tents are pitched upon the river's bank. Far away to the south we trace the dim outline of the timber on the streams flowing in from the west. Turning our eyes in that direction, we see only the level sea of verdure, — the green grass waving in the evening breeze. At this place our company will divide, — Governor Marshall, Mr. Holmes, and several other gentlemen, going on to the Missouri, while the rest of us will travel eastward to Lake Superior.

It would be a pleasure to go with them, — to ride over the rolling prairies, to fall in with buffaloes and try my pony in a race with a big bull. It would be thrilling, — only if the hunted should right about face, and toss the hunter on his horns, the thrill would be of a different sort!

We sit by our camp-fires at night with our faces and hands smeared with an abominable mixture prepared by our M. D., ostensibly to keep the mosquitoes from presenting their bills, but which we surmise is a little game of his to daub us with a diabolical mixture of glycerine, soap, and tar! Our tents are as odorous as the shop of a keeper of naval stores. There is an all-pervading smell of oakum and turpentine. Clouds of mosquitoes come, take a whiff, and retire in disgust. We can hear them having a big swear at the Doctor for compounding such an ointment!

I think of the country which those who are going west will see, and of the region beyond, — the valley of the Yellowstone, the Missouri, the slopes of the Rocky Mountains, and the hills of Montana, — territory to be included in the future Empire of the Northwest. I have written the word, but it bears no political meaning in these notes. It has the same signification as when applied to the State of New York. The Empire of the Northwest will be the territory lying north of the central ridge of the continent. Milwaukie may be taken as a starting-point for a survey of this imperial domain. That city is near the 43d parallel; following it westward, we see that it passes over the mountain-range on whose northern slopes the southern affluents of the Yellowstone take their rise. All the fertile valleys of the Columbia and its tributaries lie north of this parallel; all the streams of the Upper Missouri country, and the magnificent water-system of Puget Sound, and the intricate bays and inlets of British Columbia, reaching on to Alaska, having their only counterpart in the fiords of Norway, are north of that degree of latitude. I have already taken a view of the region now comprised in the British dominions east of the Rocky Mountains; but equally interesting will be a review of the territories of the Republic, — Dakota, Montana, Idaho, Oregon, and Washington, also British Columbia and Vancouver.

Dakota contains a little more than a hundred and fifty thousand square miles, — nearly enough territory to make four States as large as Ohio.

"The climate and soil of Dakota," says the Commissioner of Public Lands, General Wilson, in his Report for 1869, "are exceedingly favorable to the growth of wheat, corn, and other cereals, while all the fruits raised in the Northern States are here produced in the greatest perfection. . . . . The wheat crop varied from twenty to forty bushels to the acre. Oats have produced from fifty to seventy bushels to the acre, and are of excellent quality" (p. 144).

Settlements are rapidly extending up the Missouri, and another year will behold this northern section teeming with emigrants. The northern section of the territory is bare of wood, but the southern portion is well supplied with timber in the Black Hills.

Two thousand square miles of the region of the Black Hills, says Professor Hayden, geologist to the United States Exploring Expedition under

General Reynolds, is covered with excellent pine timber. That is an area half as large as the State of Connecticut, ample for the southern section; while the settlers of the northern portion will be within easy distance by rail of the timbered lands of Minnesota.

The northern half of Wyoming is north of the line we have drawn from Milwaukie to the Pacific, and of this Territory the Land Commissioner says: "A large portion of Wyoming produces a luxuriant growth of short nutritious grass, upon which cattle will feed and fatten during summer and winter without other provender. Those lands, even in their present condition, are superior for grazing. The climate is mild and healthy, the air and water pure, and springs abundant" (p. 159).

Beyond the 104th meridian lies Montana, a little larger than Dakota, with area enough for four States of the size of Ohio.

At St. Paul I was fortunate enough to fall in with Major-General Hancock, who had just returned from Montana, and who was enthusiastic in its praise.

"I consider it," he said, "to be one of the first grazing countries in the world. Its valleys are exceedingly fertile. It is capable of sustaining a dense population."

Wheat grows as luxuriantly in the valleys at the base of the Rocky Mountains as in Minnesota.

The Territory appears to be richer in minerals than any other section of the country, the gold product surpassing that of any other State or Territory. More than one hundred million dollars have been taken from the mines of Montana since the discovery of gold in this territory in 1862. Coal appears upon the Yellowstone in veins ten, fifteen, and twenty feet in thickness. It is found on the Big Horn and on the Missouri.

"From the mouth of the Big Horn," says Professor Hayden, "to the union of the Yellowstone with the Missouri, nearly all the way, lignite (coal) beds occupy the whole country. . . . . The beds are well developed, and at least twenty or thirty seams are shown, varying in purity and thickness from a few inches to seven feet" (Report, p. 59).

The mountains are covered with wood, and there will be no lack of fuel in Montana. The timber lands of this Territory are estimated by the Land Commissioner to cover nearly twelve millions of acres, — an area as large as New Hampshire and Vermont combined. The agricultural land, or land that may be ploughed, is estimated at twenty-three million acres, nearly as much as is contained in the State of Ohio. The grazing lands are put down at sixty-nine millions, — or a region as large as New York, Pennsylvania, and New Jersey together!

Is n't it cold? Are not the winters intolerable?

Are not the summers short in Montana? Many times the questions have been asked.

The temperature of the climate in winter will be seen from the following thermometrical record kept at Virginia City: —

1866.	Dec.	Mean for the month,	31°	above zero.
1867.	Jan.	" " "	23°.73	" "
"	Feb.	" " "	26°	" "

The summer climate is exceedingly agreeable, and admirably adapted to fruit culture.

In July last Mr. Milnor Roberts, Mr. Thomas Canfield, and other gentlemen of the Pacific exploring party, were in Montana. Mr. Roberts makes our mouths water by his description of the fruits of that Territory.

"Missoula," he says, "is a thriving young town near the western base of the Rocky Mountains, containing a grist-mill, saw-mill, two excellent stores, and from twenty-five to thirty dwellings, a number of them well built. I visited McWhirk's garden of five acres, where I found ripe tomatoes, watermelons, muskmelons, remarkably fine potatoes, beans, peas, and squashes; also young apple-trees and other fruit-trees, and a very fine collection of flowers; and all this had been brought about from the virgin soil in two years, and would this year (1869) yield the owner over two thousand dollars in gold, the only currency known in Montana" (Report, p. 23).

This fruit and flower garden is about one hundred miles from the top of the divide between the Atlantic and the Pacific.

Deer Lodge City, fifteen miles from the dividing ridge, is situated in the Deer Lodge Valley, and its attractions are thus set forth by Mr. Roberts: —

"The Deer Lodge Valley is very wide, in places ten to fifteen miles from the hills on one side to the hills on the other, nearly level, and everywhere clothed with rich grass, upon which we observed numerous herds of tame cattle and horses feeding. The Deer Lodge Creek flows through it, and adds immensely to its value as an agricultural region. Some farms are cultivated; but farming is yet in its infancy, and there are thousands of acres of arable land here and elsewhere in Montana awaiting settlement" (p. 25).

West of Montana is Idaho, containing eighty-six thousand square miles, — large enough for two States of the size of Ohio. Nearly all of this Territory lies north of the 43d parallel. It is watered by the Columbia and its tributaries, — mountain streams fed by melting snows.

"The mountains of Idaho," says the Land Commissioner, in his exhaustive Report for 1869, "often attain great altitude, having peaks rising above the line of perpetual snow, their lower slopes being furrowed with numerous streams and alternately clothed with magnificent forests and rich grasses.

The plains are elevated table-lands covered with indigenous grasses, constituting pasturage unsurpassed in any section of our country. Numerous large flocks of sheep and herds of domestic cattle now range these pastures, requiring but little other sustenance throughout the entire year, and no protection from the weather other than that afforded by the lower valleys or the cañons, in which many of the streams take their way through the upland country. The valleys are beautiful, fertile depressions of the surface, protected from the searching winds of summer and searching blasts of winter, each intersected by some considerable stream, adjoining which on either bank, and extending to the commencement of the rise of table-land or mountain, are broad stretches of prairies or meadows producing the richest grasses, and with the aid of irrigation, crops of grain, fruit, and vegetables superior to those of any of the Eastern States, and rivalling the vegetation of the Mississippi Valley. The pastures of these valleys are generally uncovered with snow in the most severe winters, and afford excellent food for cattle and sheep, the herbage drying upon the stalk during the later summer and autumn months into a superior quality of hay. As no artificial shelter from the weather is here required for sheep or cattle, stock-raising is attended with but little outlay and is very profitable, promising soon to become one of the greatest sources of wealth in this rapidly developing but still underrated Territory. It was considered totally valueless except for mining purposes, and uninviting to the agriculturist, until emigration disclosed its hidden resources.

"It is the favorite custom of herdsmen in Idaho to reserve their lower meadows for winter pastures, allowing the stock to range the higher plains during spring, summer, and autumn; the greater extent of the table-lands, and the superior adaptability of the valleys for agriculture presenting reasons for the adoption of this method as one of economical importance.

"The climate of Idaho varies considerably with the degrees of latitude through which its limits extend, but not so much as would naturally be supposed from its great longitudinal extension; the isothermal lines of the Territory, running from east to west, have a well-defined northward variation, caused by the influence of air currents from the Pacific Ocean. Throughout the spring, summer, and autumn months, in the northern as well as the southern sections, the weather is generally delightful and salubrious; in the winter months the range of the thermometer depends greatly upon the altitude of the surface,—the higher mountains being visited by extreme cold and by heavy falls of snow; the lower mountain-ranges and the plains having winters generally less severe than those of northern Iowa and Wisconsin or central Minnesota, while greater dryness of the atmosphere renders a lower fall of the thermometer less perceptible; and the valleys being rarely visited by cold weather, high winds, or considerable falls of snow. Considered in its yearly average, the climate is exactly adapted to sheep-growing and the production of wool, the herding of cattle, and manufacture of dairy products, the raising of very superior breeds of horses, as well as the culture of all Northern varieties of fruits, such as apples, pears, plums, cherries, peaches, grapes, and all of the ordinary cereals and vegetables" (p. 164.)

This is all different from what we have conceived the Rocky Mountains to be.

When the government reports of the explorations of 1853 were issued, Jeff Davis was Secretary of War, and he deliberately falsified the report of Governor Stevens's explorations from Lake Superior to the valley of the Columbia. Governor Stevens reported that the route passed through a region highly susceptible of agriculture; but the Secretary of War, even then plotting treason, in his summary of the advantages of the various routes, asserted that Governor Stevens had overstated the facts, and that there were not more than 1,000 square miles, or 640,000 acres, of agricultural lands. The Land Commissioner in his Report estimates the amount of agricultural lands at 16,925,000 acres. The amount of improved lands in Ohio in 1860 was 12,665,000 acres, or more than 4,000,000 less than the available agricultural lands in Idaho. These are lands that need no irrigation. Of such lands there are 14,000,000 acres, which, in the language of the Commissioner, are "redeemable by irrigation into excellent pasture and agricultural lands." The grazing-lands are estimated at 5,000,000 acres, the timbered lands at 7,500,000 acres, besides 8,000,000 acres of mineral lands. Although the population of Idaho probably does not exceed 50,000, half of whom are engaged in mining, the value of the agricultural products for 1868 amounted to $12,000,000, while the mineral product was $10,000,000.

Passing on to Oregon we find a State containing 95,000 square miles, two and a half times larger than Ohio.

"Oregon," says General Wilson, in his Report upon the public lands, "is peculiarly a crop-raising and fruit-growing State, though by no means deficient in valuable mineral resources. Possessing a climate of unrivalled salubrity, abounding in vast tracts of rich arable lands, heavily timbered throughout its mountain ranges, watered by innumerable springs and streams, and subject to none of the drawbacks arising from the chilling winds and seasons of aridity which prevail farther south, it is justly considered the most favored region on the Pacific slope as a home for an agricultural and manufacturing population" (p. 197).

Of "western Oregon," he says, "the portion of the State first settled embraces about 31,000 square miles, or 20,000,000 acres, being nearly one third of the area of the whole State, and contains the great preponderance of population and wealth. Nearly the whole of this large extent of country is valuable for agriculture and grazing; all of the productions common to temperate regions may be cultivated here with success. When the land is properly cultivated, the farmer rarely fails to meet with an adequate reward for his labors. The fruits produced here, such as apples, pears, plums, quinces, and grapes, are of superior quality and flavor. Large quantities of apples are annually shipped to the San Francisco market, where they usually command a higher price than those of California, owing to their finer flavor.

"The valleys of the Willamette, Umpqua, and Rouge Rivers, are embraced within this portion of the State, and there is no region of country on the continent presenting a finer field for agriculture and stock-raising, because of the mildness of the climate and the depth and richness of the soil. Farmers make no provision for housing their cattle during winter, and none is required; although in about the same latitude as Maine on the Atlantic, the winter temperature corresponds with that of Savannah, Georgia" (p. 194).

North of Oregon lies the Territory of Washington, containing 70,000 square miles, lacking only 9,000 to make it twice as large as Ohio.

Our camp, where I am taking this westward look, is pitched very near the 47th parallel, may be five or six miles north of it. If I were to travel due west along the parallel a little more than twelve hundred miles, I should reach Olympia, the capital of the Territory, situated on Puget Sound, — the name given to that vast ramification of waters known as the Strait of Juan de Fuca, Admiralty Inlet, Hood's Canal, and Puget Sound, with a shore line of 1,500 miles.

"There is no State in the Union," says the Land Commissioner, "and perhaps no country in the world of the same extent, that offers so many harbors and such excellent facilities for commerce" (p. 198).

The timbered lands of Washington are approximately estimated at 20,000,000 acres, and the prairie lands cover an area equally great. The forests embrace the red and yellow pine of gigantic growth, often attaining the height of three hundred feet, and from nine to twelve feet in diameter. It is said that a million feet have been cut from a single acre! Says the Commissioner, "The soil in the river-bottoms is thinly timbered with maple, ash, and willow. These lands yield heavy crops of wheat, barley, and oats, while vegetables attain enormous size. The highlands are generally rolling, and well adapted to cultivation. . . . . The average yield of potatoes to the acre is six hundred bushels, wheat forty, peas sixty, timothy-hay five tons, and oats seventy bushels" (p. 199).

Mr. Roberts, who explored this region last year, says that the great plain of the Columbia is "a high rolling prairie, covered everywhere abundantly with bunch-grass to the summits of the highest hills; treeless, excepting along the streams. This is an immense grazing area of the most superior character, interspersed with the valleys of perennial streams, along which are lands that, when settled by industrious farmers, will be of the most productive character, as we have seen in the case of a number of improvements already made; while the climate is not only salubrious, but remarkably attractive" (Report, p. 19).

He gives this estimate of the area suited to agriculture and grazing:—

"In Washington Territory alone, on its eastern side, there are at least 20,000 square miles, or 12,800,000 acres of the finest grazing-lands, on which thousands of cattle and sheep will be raised as cheaply as in any other quarter of the globe, and this grass is so nutritious that the cattle raised upon it cannot be surpassed in their weight and quality. Snow rarely falls to sufficient depth to interfere seriously with their grazing all through the winter. Such may be taken as a general view upon this important point, respecting a Territory nearly half as large as the State of Pennsylvania" (p. 19).

Along the shores of Puget Sound, and on the island of Vancouver, are extensive deposits of bituminous coal, conveniently situated for the future steam-marine of the Pacific. Large quantities are now shipped to San Francisco for the use of the Pacific mail-steamers.

Not only in Washington, but up the coast of British Columbia, the coal-deposits crop out in numerous places.

An explorer on Simpson River, which next to the Fraser is the largest in British Columbia, thus writes to Governor Douglas: "I saw seams of coal to-day fifteen feet thick, better than any mined at Vancouver" (Parliamentary Blue-Book.)

Coal in Montana, in Idaho, in Washington, on Vancouver, in British Columbia; coal on the Missouri, the Yellowstone, the Columbia, the Fraser; coal on Simpson River, coal in Alaska! Measureless forests all over the Pacific slope! timber enough for all the world, masts and spars sufficient for the mercantile marine of every nation! Great rivers, thousands of waterfalls, unequalled facilities for manufacturing! An agricultural region unsurpassed for fertility! Exhaustless mineral wealth! Fisheries equalling those of Newfoundland, — salmon in every stream, cod and herring abounding along the coast! Nothing wanting for a varied industry.

Unfold the map of North America and look at its western coast. From Panama northward there is no harbor that can ever be available to the commerce of the Pacific till we reach the Bay of San Francisco. From thence northward to the Columbia the waves of the sea break against rugged mountains. The Columbia pours its waters through the Coast Range, but a bar at its mouth has practically closed it to commerce. Not till we reach Puget Sound do we find a good harbor. North of that magnificent gateway are numberless bays and inlets. Like the coast of Maine, there is a harbor every five or ten miles, where ships may ride in safety, sheltered from storms, and open at all seasons of the year. There never will be any icebound ships on the coast of British Columbia, for the warm breath of the tropics is felt there throughout the year.

While the map is unfolded, look at Puget Sound, and think of its connection with Japan and China. Latitude and longitude are to be taken into account when we make long journeys. Liverpool is between the 53d and 54th parallels, or about two hundred and sixty miles farther north than Puget Sound, where a degree of longitude is only thirty-five miles in length. Puget Sound is on the 49th parallel, where the degrees are thirty-eight and a half miles in length. San Francisco is near the 37th parallel, where the degrees are nearly forty-nine miles in length. Liverpool is three degrees west of Greenwich, from which longitude is reckoned. The 122d meridian passes through Puget Sound and also through the Bay of San Francisco. It follows from all this that the distance from Liverpool in straight lines to these two magnificent gateways of the Pacific, in geographical miles, is as follows: —

Liverpool to San Francisco .	4,879	miles.
" " Puget Sound . .	4,487	"
Difference,	392	"

Looking across the Pacific we see that Yokohama is on the 35th parallel, where a degree of longitude is forty-nine miles in length. Reckoning the distance across the Pacific between Yokohama and the western gateways of the continent, we have this comparison : —

San Francisco to Yokohama .	4,856	miles.
Puget Sound " " . .	4,294	"
Difference,	562	"

Adding these differences together, we see that longitude alone makes a total of nine hundred and fifty-four miles in favor of Puget Sound between Liverpool and Yokohama. When the Northern Pacific Railroad is completed, Chicago will be fully six hundred miles nearer Asia by Puget Sound than by San Francisco.

Vessels sailing from Japan to San Francisco follow the Kuro-Siwo, the heated river, which of itself bears them towards Puget Sound at the rate of eighty miles a day. They follow it into northern latitudes till within three or four hundred miles of the coast of British Columbia, then shape their course southward past Puget Sound to the Golden Gate.

In navigation, then, Asia is nearly, if not quite, one thousand miles nearer the ports of Puget Sound than San Francisco. The time will come when not only Puget Sound, but every bay and inlet of the northwest coast, will be whitened with sails of vessels bringing the products of the Orient, not only for those who dwell upon the Pacific slope, but for the mighty multitude of the Empire of the Northwest, of the Mississippi Valley, and the Atlantic States.

From those land-locked harbors steamships shall depart for other climes, freighted with the products of this region, spun and woven, hammered and smelted, sawed and planed, by the millions of industrious workers who are to improve the unparalleled capabilities of this vast domain.

There is not on the face of the globe a country so richly endowed as this of the Northwest. Here we find every element necessary for the development of a varied industry, — agricultural, mining, manufacturing, mercantile, and commercial, — all this with a climate like that of southern France, or central and northern Europe.

"The climate," says Mr. Roberts, "of this favored region is very remarkable, and will always remain an attractive feature; which must, therefore, aid greatly in the speedy settlement of this portion of the Pacific coast. Even in the coldest winters there is practically no obstruction to navigation from ice; vessels can enter and depart at all times; and the winters are so mild that summer flowers which in the latitude of Philadelphia, on the Atlantic coast, we are obliged to place in the hot-house, are left out in the open garden without being injured. The cause of this mildness is usually, and I think correctly, ascribed to the warm-water equatorial current, which, impinging against the Pacific coast, north of the Strait of Juan de Fuca, passes along nearly parallel with the shore, diffusing its genial warmth over the land far into the interior. Of the fact there is no doubt, whatever may be the cause" (Report, p. 14).

The climate of eastern Washington, amid the mountains, corresponds with that of Pennsylvania; but upon the sea-coast and along the waters of Puget Sound roses blossom in the open air throughout the year, and the residents gather green peas and strawberries in March and April.

In a former view we looked at the territory belonging to Great Britain lying east of the Rocky Mountains, we saw its capabilities for settlement; but far different in its physical features is British Columbia from the Saskatchawan country. It is a land of mountains, plains, valleys, and forests, threaded by rivers, and indented by bays and inlets. The main branch of the Columbia rises in the British Possessions, between the Cascade Range and the Rocky Mountains. There is a great amphitheatre between those two ranges, having an area of forty-five thousand square miles. We hardly comprehend, even with a map spread out before us, that there is an area larger than Ohio in the basin drained by the northern branch of the Columbia. But such is the fact, and it is represented as being a fertile and attractive section, possessed of a mild and equable climate. The stock-raisers of southern Idaho drive their cattle by the ten thousand into British Columbia to find winter pasturage!

The general characteristics of that area have been fully set forth in a paper read before the Royal

Geographical Society of London by Lieutenant Palmer of the Royal Engineers. He says: —

"The scenery of the whole midland belt, especially of that portion of it lying to the east of the 124th meridian, is exceedingly beautiful and picturesque. The highest uplands are all more or less thickly timbered, but the valleys present a delightful panorama of woodland and prairie, flanked by miles of rolling hills, swelling gently from the margin of streams, and picturesquely dotted with yellow pines. The forests are almost entirely free from underwood, and with the exception of a few worthless tracts, the whole face of the country — hill and dale, woodland and plain — is covered with an abundant growth of grass, possessing nutritious qualities of the highest order. Hence its value to the colony as a grazing district is of the highest importance. Cattle and horses are found to thrive wonderfully on the 'bunch' grass, and to keep in excellent condition at all seasons. The whole area is more or less available for grazing purposes. Thus the natural pastures of the middle belt may be estimated at hundreds, or even thousands, of square miles.

"Notwithstanding the elevation, the seasons exhibit no remarkable extremes of temperature; the winters, though sharp enough for all the rivers and lakes to freeze, are calm and clear, so that the cold, even when most severe, is not keenly felt. Snow seldom exceeds eighteen inches in depth, and in many valleys of moderate elevation cattle often range at large during the winter months, without requiring shelter or any food but the natural grasses. . . . . Judging from present experience, there can be no doubt that in point of salubrity the climate of British Columbia excels that of Great Britain, and is indeed one of the finest in the world."

In regard to the agricultural capabilities of this mountain region, the same author remarks: —

"Here in sheltered and well-irrigated valleys, at altitudes of as much as 2,500 feet above the sea, a few farming experiments have been made, and the results have thus far been beyond measure encouraging. At farms in the San José and Beaver valleys, situated nearly 2,200 feet above the sea, and again at Fort Alexander, at an altitude of 1,450 feet, wheat has been found to produce nearly forty bushels to the acre, and other grain and vegetable crops in proportion. . . . . It may be asserted that two thirds at least of this eastern division of the central belt may, when occasion arrives, be turned to good account either for purposes of grazing or tillage."

Probably there are no streams, bays, or inlets in the world that so abound with fish as the salt and fresh waters of the northwest Pacific. The cod and herring fisheries are equal to those of Newfoundland, while every stream descending from the mountains literally swarms with salmon.

In regard to the fisheries of British Columbia, Lieutenant Palmer says: —

"The whole of the inlets, bays, rivers, and lakes of British Columbia abound with delicious fish. The quantity of salmon that ascend the Fraser and other rivers on the coast seems incredible. They first enter Fraser and other rivers in March, and are followed in rapid succession by other varieties, which continue to arrive until the approach of winter; but the great runs occur in July, August, and September. During these months so abundant is the supply that it may be asserted without exaggeration, that some of the smaller streams can hardly be forded without stepping upon them." (Journal of the Geographical Society.)

Ah! would n't it be glorious sport to pull out the twenty-five-pounders from the foaming waters of the Columbia, — to land them, one after another, on the grassy bank, and see the changing light upon their shining scales! and then sitting down to dinner to have one of the biggest on a platter, delicately baked or boiled, with prairie chicken, plover, pigeon, and wild duck! We will have it by and by, when Governor Smith and Judge Rice, who are out here seeing about the railroad, get the cars running to the Pacific; they will supply all creation east of the Rocky Mountains with salmon!

There are not many of us who can afford to dine off salmon when it is a dollar a pound, and the larger part of the crowd can never have a taste even; but these railroad gentlemen will bring about a new order of things. When they get the locomotive on the completed track, and make the run from the Columbia to Chicago in about sixty hours, as they will be able to do, all hands of us who work for our daily bread will be able to have fresh salmon at cheap rates.

What a country! I have drawn a hypothetical line from Milwaukie to the Pacific, — not that the region south of it — Missouri, Kansas, Nebraska, or California — does not abound in natural resources, with fruitful soil and vast capabilities, but because the configuration of the continent — the water-systems, the mountain-ranges, the elevations and depressions, the soil and climate — is in many respects different north of the 43d parallel from what it is south of it. We need not look upon the territory now held by Great Britain with a covetous eye. The 49th parallel is an imaginary line running across the prairies, an arbitrary political boundary which Nature will not take into account in her disposition of affairs in the future. Sooner or later the line will fade away. Railway trains — the constant passing and repassing of a multitude of people speaking the same language, having ideas in common, and related by blood —

will rub it out, and there will be one country, one people, one government. What an empire then! The region west of Lake Michigan and north of the latitude of Milwaukie — the 43d parallel extended to the Pacific — will give to the nation, to say nothing of Alaska Territory, forty States as large as Ohio, or two hundred States of the size of Massachusetts!

I have been accustomed to look upon this part of the world as being so far north, so cold, so snowy, so distant, — and all the other imaginary so's, — that it never could be available for settlement; but the facts show that it is as capable of settlement as New York or New England, — that the country along the Athabasca has a climate no more severe than that of northern New Hampshire or Maine, while the summers are more favorable to the growing of grains than those of the northern Atlantic coast.

It is not, therefore, hypothetical geography. Following the 43d parallel eastward, we find it passing along the northern shore of the Mediterranean, through central Italy, and through the heart of the Turkish Empire. Nearly all of Europe lies north of it, — the whole of France, half of Italy, the whole of the Austrian Empire, and all of Russia's vast dominions.

The entire wheat-field of Europe is above that parallel. The valleys of the Alps lying between the 46th and 50th parallels swarm with an industrious people; why may not those of the Rocky Mountains at the head-waters of the Missouri and Columbia in like manner be hives of industry in the future?

If a Christiania, a Stockholm, and a St. Petersburg, with golden-domed churches, gorgeous palaces, and abodes of comfort, can be built up in lat. 60 in the Old World, why may we not expect to see their counterpart in the New, when we take into account the fact that a heated current from the tropics gives the same mildness of climate to the northwestern section of this continent that the Gulf Stream gives to northern Europe?

With this outlook towards future possibilities, we see Minnesota the central State of the Continental Republic of the future.

With the map of the continent before me, I stick a pin into Minneapolis, and stretch a string to Halifax, then, sweeping southward, find that it cuts through southern Florida, and central Mexico. It reaches almost to San Diego, the extreme southwestern boundary of the United States, — reaches to Donner Pass on the summit of the Sierra Nevadas, within a hundred miles of Sacramento. Stretching it due west, it reaches to Salem, Oregon. Carrying it northwest, I find that it reaches to the Rocky Mountain House on Peace

River, — to that region whose beauty charmed Mackenzie and Father De Smet. The Peace River flows through the Rocky Mountains, and at its head-waters we find the lowest pass of the continent. The time may come when we of the East will whirl through it upon the express-train bound for Sitka! It is two hundred miles from the Rocky Mountain House to that port of southern Alaska.

The city of Mexico is nearer Minneapolis by nearly a hundred miles than Sitka. Trinity Bay on the eastern coast of Newfoundland, Puerto Principe on the island of Cuba, the Bay of Honduras in Central America, and Sitka, are equidistant from Minneapolis and St. Paul.

When Mr. Seward, in 1860, addressed the people of St. Paul from the steps of the Capitol, it was the seer, and not the politician, who said: —

"*I now believe that the ultimate last seat of government on this great continent will be found somewhere within a circle or radius not far from the spot on which I stand, at the head of navigation on the Mississippi River!*"

CHAPTER V.

THE FRONTIER.

BOTTINEAU is our guide. Take a look at him as he sits by the camp-fire cleaning his rifle. He is tall and well formed, with features which show both his French and Indian parentage. He has dark whiskers, a broad, flat nose, a wrinkled forehead, and is in the full prime of life. His name is known throughout the Northwest, — among Americans, Canadians, and Indians. The Chippewa is his mother-tongue, though he can speak several Indian dialects, and is fluent in French and English. He was born not far from Fort Garry, and has traversed the vast region of the Northwest in every direction. He was Governor Stevens's guide when he made the first explorations for the Northern Pacific Railroad, and has guided a great many government trains to the forts on the Missouri since then. He was with General Sully in his campaign against the Indians. He has the instinct of locality. Like the honey-bee, which flies straight from the flower to its hive, over fields, through forests, across ravines or intervening hills, so Pierre Bottineau knows just where to go when out upon the boundless prairie with no landmark to guide him. He is never lost, even in the darkest night or foggiest day.

There is no man living, probably, who has more enemies than he, for the whole Sioux nation of Indians are his sworn foes. They would take his scalp instantly if they could only get a chance. He has been in many fights with them, — has killed six of them, has had narrow escapes, and to hear him tell of his adventures makes your hair stand on end. He is going to conduct a portion of our party through the Sioux country. The Indians are friendly now, and the party will not be troubled; but if a Sioux buffalo-hunter comes across this guide there will be quick shooting on both sides, and ten to one the Indian will go down, — for Bottineau is keen-sighted, has a steady hand, and is quick to act.

The westward-bound members of our party, guided by Bottineau, will be accompanied by an escort consisting of nineteen soldiers commanded by Lieutenant Kelton. Four Indian scouts, mounted on ponies, are engaged to scour the country in advance, and give timely notice of the presence of Sioux, who are always on the alert to steal horses or plunder a train.

Bidding our friends good by, we watch their train winding over the prairie till we can only see the white canvas of the wagons on the edge of the horizon; then, turning eastward, we cross the river into Minnesota, and strike out upon the pathless plain. We see no landmarks ahead, and, like navigators upon the ocean, pursue our way over this sea of verdure by the compass.

After a few hours' ride, we catch, through the glimmering haze, the faint outlines of islands rising above the unruffled waters of a distant lake. We approach its shores, but only to see islands and lake alike vanish into thin air. It was the mirage lifting above the horizon the far-off groves of Buffalo Creek, a branch of the Red River.

Far away to the east are the Leaf Hills, which are only the elevations of the rolling prairie that forms the divide between the waters flowing into the Gulf of Mexico and into Hudson Bay.

Wishing to see the hills, to ascertain what obstacles there are to the construction of a railroad, two of us break away from the main party and strike out over the plains, promising to be in camp at nightfall. How exhilarating to gallop over the pathless expanse, amid a sea of flowers, plunging now and then through grass so high that horse and rider are almost lost to sight! The meadow-lark greets us with his cheerful song; the plover hovers around us; sand-hill cranes, flying always in pairs, rise from the ground and wing their way beyond the reach of harm. The gophers chatter like children amid the flowers, as we ride over their subterranean towns.

They are in peaceful possession of the solitude. Five years ago buffaloes were roaming here. We see their bones bleaching in the sun. Here the Sioux and Chippewas hunted them down. Here the old bulls fought out their battles, and the countless herds cropped the succulent grasses and drank the clear running water of the stream which bears their name. They are gone forever. The ox and cow of the farm are coming to take their place. Sheep and horses will soon fatten on the rich pasturage of these hills. We of the East would hardly call them hills, much less mountains, the slopes are so gentle and the altitudes so low. The highest grade of a railroad would not exceed thirty feet to the mile in crossing them.

Here we find granite and limestone bowlders, and in some places beds of gravel, brought, so the geologists inform us, from the far North and deposited here when the primeval ocean currents set southward over this then submerged region. They are in the right place for the railroad. The stone will be needed for abutments to bridges, and the gravel will be wanted for ballast, — provided the road is located in this vicinity.

On our second day's march we come to what might with propriety be called the park region of Minnesota. It lies amid the high lands of the divide. It is more beautiful even than the country around White Bear Lake and in the vicinity of Glenwood. Throughout the day we behold such rural scenery as can only be found amid the most lovely spots in England.

Think of rounded hills, with green slopes, — of parks and countless lakes, — skirted by forests, fringed with rushes, perfumed by tiger-lilies — the waves rippling on gravelled beaches; wild geese, ducks, loons, pelicans, and innumerable water-fowl building their nests amid the reeds and rushes, — think of lawns blooming with flowers, elk and deer browsing in the verdant meadows. This is their haunt. We see their tracks along the sandy shores, but they keep beyond the range of our rifles.

So wonderfully has nature adorned this section, that it seems as if we were riding through a country that has been long under cultivation, and that behind yonder hillock we shall find an old castle, a mansion, or, at least, a farm-house, as we find them in Great Britain.

I do not forget that I am seeing Minnesota at its best season, that it is midsummer, that the winters are as long as in New England; but I can say without reservation, that nowhere in the wide world — not even in old England, the most finished of all lands; not in *la belle France,* or sunny Italy, or in the valley of the Ganges or the Yangtse, or on the slopes of the Sierra Nevadas — have I beheld anything approaching this in natural beauty.

How it would look in winter I cannot say, but

the members of our party are unanimous in their praises of this portion of Minnesota. The nearest pioneer is forty miles distant; but land so inviting will soon be taken up by settlers.

It was a pleasure, after three days' travel over the trackless wild, to come suddenly and unexpectedly upon a hay-field. There were the swaths newly mown. There was no farm-house in sight, no fenced area or upturned furrow, but the haymakers had been there. We were approaching civilization once more. Ascending a hill, we came in sight of a settler, a pioneer who is always on the move; who, when a neighbor comes within six or eight miles of him, abandons his home and moves on to some spot where he can have more elbow-room, — to a region not so thickly peopled.

He informed us that we should find the old trail we were searching for about a mile ahead. He had long matted hair, beard hanging upon his breast, a wrinkled countenance, wore a slouched felt hat, an old checked-cotton shirt, and pantaloons so patched and darned, so variegated in color, that it would require much study to determine what was original texture and what patch and darn. He came from Ohio in his youth, and has always been a skirmisher on the advancing line of civilization, — a few miles ahead of the main body. He was thinking now of going into the "bush," as he phrased it.

Settlers farther down the trail informed us that he was a little flighty and queer; that he could not be induced to stay long in one place, but was always on the move for a more quiet neighborhood!

The road that we reached at this point was formerly traversed by the French and Indian traders between Pembina and the Mississippi, but has not been used much of late years. Striking that, we should have no difficulty in reaching the settlements of the Otter-Tail, forty miles south.

Emigration travels fast. As fires blown by winds sweep through the dried grass of the prairies, so civilization spreads along the frontier.

We reached the settlement on Saturday night, and pitched our tents for the Sabbath. It was a rare treat to these people to come into our camp and hear a sermon from Rev. Dr. Lord. The oldest member of the colony is a woman, now in her eightieth year, with eye undimmed and a countenance remarkably free from the marks of age, who walks with a firm step after fourscore years of labor. Sixty years ago she moved from Lebanon, New Hampshire, a young wife, leaving the valley of the Connecticut for a home in the State of New York, then moving with the great army of emigrants to Ohio, Illinois, Missouri, and Iowa in succession, and now beginning again in Minnesota. Last year her hair, which had been as white as the purest snow, began to take on its original color, and is now quite dark! There are but few instances on record of such a renewal of youth.

The party have come from central Iowa to make this their future home, preferring the climate of this region, where the changes of temperature are not so sudden and variable. The women and children of the four families lived here alone for six weeks, while the men were away after their stock. Their nearest neighbors are twelve miles distant. On the 4th of July all hands — men, women, and children — travelled forty-five miles to celebrate the day.

"We felt," said one of the women, "that we could n't get through the year without going somewhere or seeing somebody. It is kinder lonely so far away from folks, and so we went down country to a picnic."

Store, church, and school are all forty miles away, and till recently the nearest saw-mill was sixty miles distant. Now they can get their wheat ground by going forty miles.

The settlement is already blooming with half a dozen children. Other emigrants are coming, and these people are looking forward to next year with hope and confidence, for then they will have a school of their own.

In our march south from Detroit Lake we meet a large number of Chippewa Indians going to the Reservation recently assigned them by the government in one of the fairest sections of Minnesota. Among them we see several women with blue eyes and light hair and fair complexions, who have French blood in their veins, and possibly some of them may have had American fathers. Nearly all of the Indians wear pantaloons and jackets; but here and there we see a brave who is true to his ancestry, who is proud of his lineage and race, and is in all respects a savage, in moccasons, blanket, skunk-skin head-dress, and painted eagle's feathers.

They are friendly, inoffensive, and indolent, and took no part in the late war. They have been in close contact with the whites for a long time, but they do not advance in civilization. All efforts for their elevation are like rain-drops falling on a cabbage-leaf, that roll off and leave it dry. There is little absorption on the part of the Indians except of whiskey, and in that respect their powers are great, — equal to those of the driest toper in Boston or anywhere else devoting all his energies to getting round the Prohibitory Law.

Our halting-place for Monday night is on the bank of the Otter-Tail, near Rush Lake. The tents are pitched, the camp-fire kindled, supper eaten, and we are sitting before a pile of blazing logs. The dew is falling, and the fire is comfortable and social. We look into the glowing coals and think of old times, and of friends far away.

We dream of home. Then the jest and the story go round. The song would follow if we had the singers. But music is not wanting. We hear martial strains,—of cornets, trombones, ophicleides, and horns, and the beating of a drum. Torches gleam upon the horizon, and by their flickering light we see a band advancing over the prairie. It is a march of welcome to the Northern Pacific Exploring Party.

Not an hour ago these musicians heard of our arrival, and here they are, twelve of them, in our camp, doing their best to express their joy. They are Germans,—all young men. Three years ago several families came here from Ohio. They reported the soil so fertile, the situation so attractive, the prospects so flattering, that others came; and now they have a dozen families, and more are coming to this land of promise.

Take a good long look at these men as they stand before our camp-fire, with their bright new instruments in their hands. They received them only three weeks ago from Cincinnati.

"We can't play much yet," says the leader, Mr. Bertenheimer, "but we do the best we can. We have sent to Toledo for a teacher who will spend the winter with us. You will pardon our poor playing, but we felt so good when we heard you were here looking out a route for a railroad, that we felt like doing something to show our goodwill. You see we are just getting started, and have to work hard, but we wanted some recreation, and we concluded to get up a band. We thought it would be better than to be hanging round a grocery. We have n't any grocery yet, and if we keep sober, and give our attention to other things, perhaps we sha' n't have one, — which, I reckon, will be all the better for us."

Plain and simple the words, but there is more in them than in many a windy speech made on the rostrum or in legislative halls. Just getting started! Yet here upon the frontier Art has planted herself. The flowers of civilization are blooming on the border.

As we listen to the parting strains, and watch the receding forms, and look into the coals of our camp-fire after their departure, we feel that there must be a bright future for a commonwealth that can grow such fruit on the borders of the uncultivated wilderness.

Now just ride out and see what has been done by these emigrants. Here is a field containing thirty acres of as fine wheat as grows in Minnesota. It is just taking on the golden hue, and will be ready for the reaper next week. Beside it are twenty acres of oats, several acres of corn, an acre or two of potatoes. This is one farm only. On yonder slope there stands a two-storied house, of hewn logs and shingled roof. See what adornment the wife or daughter has given to the front yard, — verbenas, petunias, and nasturtiums, and round the door a living wreath of morning-glories.

Cows chew their cud in the stable-yard, while

"Drowsy tinklings lull the distant field"

where the sheep are herded.

We shall find the scene repeated on the adjoining farm. Sheltered beneath the grand old forest-trees stands the little log church with a cross upon its roof, and here we see coming down the road the venerable father and teacher of the community, in long black gown and broad-brimmed hat, with a crucifix at his girdle. It is a Catholic community, and they brought their priest with them.

In the morning we ride over smiling prairies, through groves of oak and maple, and behold in the distance a large territory covered with the lithe foliage of the tamarack. Here and there are groves of pine rising like islands above the wide level of the forest.

At times our horses walk on pebbly beaches and splash their hoofs in the limpid waters of the lakes. We pick up agates, carnelians, and bits of bright red porphyry, washed and worn by the waves. Wild swans rear their young in the reeds and marshes bordering the streams. They gracefully glide over the still waters. They are beyond the reach of our rifles, and we would not harm them if we could. There is a good deal of the savage left in a man who, under the plea of sport, can wound or kill a harmless bird or beast that cannot be made to serve his wants. It gives me pleasure to say that our party are not blood-thirsty. Ducks, plover, snipe, wild geese, and sand-hill cranes are served at our table, but they are never shot in wanton spot.

The stream which we have crossed several times is the Otter-Tail and flows southward into Otter-Tail Lake; issuing from that it runs southwest, then west, then northward, taking the name of the Red River, and pours its waters into Lake Winnipeg. From that great northern reservoir the waters of this western region of Minnesota reach Hudson Bay through Nelson River.

Looking eastward we see gleaming in the morning sunlight the Leaf Lakes, the head-waters of the Crow-Wing, one of the largest western tributaries of the Upper Mississippi.

The neck of land between these lakes and the Otter-Tail is only one mile wide. Here, from time out of mind among the Indians, the transit has been made between the waters flowing into the Gulf of Mexico and into Hudson Bay. When the Jesuit missionaries came here, they found it the great Indian carrying-place.

Mackenzie, Lord Selkirk, and all the early adventurers, came by this route on their way to British America. For a long time it has been a trading-post. The French Jesuit fathers were here a century ago and are here to-day, — not spiritual fathers alone, but according to the flesh as well! The settlement is composed wholly of French Canadians, their Indian wives and copper-colored children. There are ten or a dozen houses, but they are very dilapidated. A little old man with twinkling gray eyes, wearing a battered white hat, comes out to welcome us, while crowds of swarthy children and Indian women gaze at us from the doorways. Another little old man, in a black gown and broad-brimmed hat, with a long chain and crucifix dangling from his girdle, salutes us with true French politeness. He is the priest, and is as seedy as the village itself.

Around the place are several birch-bark Indian huts, and a few lodges of tanned buffalo-hides. Filth, squalor, and degradation are the characteristics of the lodge, and the civilization of the log-houses is but little removed from that of the wigwams.

The French Canadian takes about as readily to the Indian maiden as to one of his own race. He is kinder than the Indian brave, and when he wants a wife he will find the fairest of the maidens ready to listen to his words of love.

CHAPTER VI.

ROUND THE CAMP-FIRE.

OUR halting-place at noon furnishes a pleasing subject for a comic artist. Behold us beneath the shade of old oaks, our horses cropping the rank grass, a fire kindled against the trunk of a tree that has braved the storms of centuries, each toasting a slice of salt pork.

Governor, members of Congress, minister, judge, doctor, teamster, correspondent, — all hands are at it. Salt pork! Does any one turn up his nose at it? Do you think it hard fare? Just come out here and try it, after a twenty-five-mile gallop on horseback, in this clear, bracing atmosphere, with twenty more miles to make before getting into camp. We slept in a tent last night; had breakfast at 5 A. M.; are camping by night and tramping by day; are bronzed by the sun; and are roughing it! The exercise of the day gives sweet sleep at night. We had a good appetite at breakfast, and now, at noon, are as hungry as bears. Salt pork is not of much account in a down-town eating-house, but out here it is epicurean fare.

Just see the Ex-Governor of the Green Mountain State standing before the fire with a long stick in his hand, having three prongs like Neptune's trident. He is doing his pork to a beautiful brown. Now he lays it between two slices of bread, and eats it as if it were a most delicious morsel, — as it is.

A dozen toasting-forks are held up to the glowing coals. A dozen slices of pork are sizzling. We are not all of us quite so scientific in our toasting as the Ex-Governor in his.

Although I have had camp-life before, and have fried flapjacks on an old iron shovel, I am subject to mishaps. There goes my pork into the ashes; never mind! I shall need less pepper. I job my trident into the slice, — flaming now, and turning to crisp, — hold it a moment before the coals, and slap it on my bread in season to save a little of the drip.

Do I hear some one exclaim, How can he eat it? Ah! you who never have had experience on the prairies don't know the pleasures of such a lunch.

Now, because we are all as jolly as we can be, because I have praised salt pork, I would n't have everybody rushing out here to try it, as they have rushed to the Adirondacks, fired to a high pitch of enthusiasm by the spirited descriptions of the pleasures of the wilderness by the pastor of the Boston Park Street Church. What is sweet to me may be sour to somebody else. I should not like this manner of life all the time, nor salt pork for a steady diet.

Wooded prairies, oak openings, hills and vales, watered by lakes and ponds, — such is the character of the region lying south of Otter-Tail. Over all this section the water is as pure as that gurgling from the hillsides of New Hampshire.

Minnesota is one of the best-watered States of the Union. The thousands of lakes and ponds dotting its surface are fed by never-failing springs. This one feature adds immeasurably to its value as an agricultural State. In Illinois, Iowa, and Nebraska the farmer is compelled to pump water for his stock, and in those States we see windmills erected for that purpose; but here the ponds are so numerous and the springs so abundant that far less pumping will be required than in the other prairie States of the Union.

We fall in with a Dutchman, where we camp for the night, who has taken up a hundred and sixty acres under the Pre-emption Act. He has put up a log-hut, turned a few acres of the sod, and is getting ready to live. His thrifty wife has a flock of hens, which supply us with fresh eggs. This pioneer has recently come from Montana. He had a beautiful farm in the Deer Lodge Pass of the Rocky Mountains, within seven miles of the summit.

"I raised as good wheat there as I can here," he says, — "thirty bushels to the acre."

"Why did you leave it?"

"I could n't sell anything. There is no market there. The farmers raise so much that they can hardly give their grain away."

"Did you sell your farm?"

"No, I left it. It is there for anybody to take."

"Is it cold there?"

"No colder than it is here. We have a few cold days in winter, but not much snow. Cattle live in the fields through the winter, feeding on bunch-grass, which grows tall and is very sweet."

Here was information worth having, — the experience of a farmer. The Deer Lodge Pass is at the head-waters of the Missouri, in the main divide of the Rocky Mountains, and one of the surveyed lines of the Northern Pacific Railroad passes through it. We have thought of it as a place where a railroad train would be frozen up and buried beneath descending avalanches; but here is a man who has lived within seven miles of the top of the mountains, who raised the best of wheat, the mealiest of potatoes, whose cattle lived in the pastures through the winter, but who left his farm for the sole reason that he could not sell anything. Montana has no market except among the mining population, and the miners are scattered over a vast region. A few farmers in the vicinity of a mining-camp supply the wants of the place. Farming will not be remunerative till a railroad is completed up the valley of the Yellowstone or

TOASTING PORK.

Missouri. What stronger argument can there be, what demonstration more forcible, for the immediate construction of the Northern Pacific Railroad? It will pass through the heart of the Territory which is yielding more gold and silver than any other Territory or State.

This farmer says that Montana is destined to be a great stock-growing State. Cattle thrive on the bunch-grass. The hills are covered with it, and millions of acres that cannot be readily cultivated will furnish pasturage for flocks and herds. This testimony accords with statements made by those who have visited the Territory, as well as by others who have resided there.

We have met to-day a long train of wagons filled with emigrants, who have come from Wisconsin, Illinois, Indiana, and some from Ohio.

Look at the wagons, each drawn by four oxen,—driven either by the owner or one of his barefoot boys. Boxes, barrels, chairs, tables, pots, and pans constitute the furniture. The grandmother, white-haired, old, and wrinkled, and the wife with an infant in her arms, with three or four romping children around her, all sitting on a feather-bed beneath the white canvas covering. A tin kettle is suspended beneath the axle, in which a tow-headed urchin, covered with dust, is swinging, clapping his hands, and playing with a yellow dog trotting behind the team. A hoop-skirt, a chicken-coop, a pig in a box, are the most conspicuous objects that meet the eye as we look at the hinder part of the wagon. A barefooted boy, as bright-eyed as Whittier's ideal, — now done in chromo-lithograph, and adorning many a home, — marches behind, with his rosy-cheeked sister, driving a cow and a calf.

To-night they will be fifteen miles nearer their destination than they were in the morning. Some of the teams have been two months on the road, and a few more days will bring them to the spot which the emigrant has already selected for his future home. They halt by the roadside at night. The oxen crop the rich grasses; the cow supplies the little ones with milk; the children gather an armful of sticks, the mother makes a cake, and bakes it before the camp-fire in a tin baker such as was found in every New England home forty years ago; the emigrant smokes his pipe, rolls himself in a blanket, and snores upon the ground beneath the wagon, while his family sleep equally well beneath the canvas roof above him. Another cake in the morning, with a slice of fried pork, a drink of coffee, and they are ready for the new day.

Not only along this road, but everywhere, we may behold just such scenes. A great army of occupation is moving into the State. The advance is all along the line. Towns and villages are springing up as if by magic in every county.

Every day adds thousands of acres to those already under cultivation. The fields of this year are wider than they were a year ago, and twelve months hence will be much larger than they are to-day.

In all new countries, no matter how fertile they may be, breadstuffs must be imported at the outset. It was so when California was first settled; but to-day California is sending her wheat all over the world. The first settlers of Minnesota were lumbermen, and up to 1857 there was not wheat enough produced in the State to supply their wants. The steamers ascending the Mississippi to St. Paul were loaded with flour, and the world at large somehow came to think of Minnesota as being so cold that wheat enough to supply the few lumbermen employed in the forests and on the rivers could never be raised there.

See how this region, which we all thought of as lying too near the north pole to be worth anything, has developed its resources! In 1854 the number of acres under cultivation in the State was only fifteen thousand, or about two thirds of a single township.

Fifteen years have passed by, and the tilled area is estimated at about two million acres! In 1857 she imported grain; but her yield of wheat the present year is estimated *at more than twenty million bushels!*

I would not make the farmers of New England

discontented. I would not advise all to put up their farms at auction, or any well-to-do farmer of Massachusetts or Vermont to leave his old home and rush out here without first coming to survey the country; but if I were a young man selling corsets and hoop-skirts to simpering young ladies in a city store, I would give such a jump over the counter that my feet would touch ground in the centre of a great prairie!

I would have a homestead out here. True, there would be hard fare at first. The cabin would be of logs. There would be short commons for a year or two. But with my salt pork I would have pickerel, prairie chickens, moose, and deer. I should have calloused hands and the back-ache at times; but my sleep would be sweet. I should have no theatre to visit nightly, no star actors to see, and should miss the tramp of the great multitude of the city, — the ever-hurrying throng. The first year might be lonely; possibly, I should have the blues now and then; but, possessing my soul with patience a twelvemonth, I should have neighbors. The railroad would come. The little log-hut would give place to a mansion. Roses would bloom in the garden, and morning-glories open their blue bells by the doorway. The vast expanse would wave with golden grain. Thrift and plenty, and civilization with all its comforts and luxuries, would be mine.

Are the colors of the picture too bright? Remember that in 1849 Minnesota had less than five thousand inhabitants, and that to-day she has nearly five hundred thousand.

I am writing to young men who have the whole scope of life before them. You are a clerk in a store, with a salary of five hundred dollars, perhaps seven hundred. By stinting here and there you can just bring the year round. It is a long, long look ahead, and your brightest day-dream of the future is not very bright.

Now take a look in this direction. You can get a hundred and sixty acres of land for two hundred dollars. If you obtain it near a railroad, it will cost three hundred and twenty dollars. It will cost three dollars an acre to plough the ground and prepare it for the first crop, besides the fencing. But the first crop, ordinarily, will more than pay the entire outlay for ground, fencing, and ploughing. Five years hence the land will be worth fifteen or twenty-five dollars per acre. This is no fancy sketch. It is simply a statement as to what has been the experience of thousands of people in Minnesota.

Think of it, young men, you who are rubbing along from year to year with no great hopes for the future. Can you hold a plough? Can you drive a span of horses? Can you accept for a while the solitude of nature, and have a few hard knocks for a year or two? Can you lay aside paper collars and kid gloves, and wear a blue blouse and blister your hands with work? Can you possess your soul in patience, and hold on your way with a firm purpose? If you can, there is a beautiful home for you out here. Prosperity, freedom, independence, manhood in its highest sense, peace of mind, and all the comforts and luxuries of life, are awaiting you.

There is no medicine for a wearied mind or jaded body equal to life on the prairies. When our party left the East, every member of it was worn down by hard work. Some of us were dyspeptic, some nervous, while others had tired brains. It is the misfortune of Americans to be ever working as if they were in the iron-mills, or as if the Philistines had them in the prison-house!

We have been a few weeks upon the frontier, — been beyond the reach of the daily newspaper, beyond care and trouble. The world has got on without us, and now we are on our way back, changed beings. We are as good as new, — tough, rugged, hale, hearty, and ready for a frolic here, or another battle with life when we reach home.

Behold us at our halting-place for the night; a clear stream near by winding through pleasant meadows, bordered by oaks and maples. The horses are unharnessed, and are rolling in the tall grass after their long day's work. The teamsters are pitching the tents, the cook is busy with his pots and kettles. Already we inhale the aroma steaming from the nose of the coffee-pot. The pork and fish and plover over the fire, like a missionary or colporteur or Sunday-school teacher, are doing good! What odor more refreshing than that exhaled from a coffee-pot steaming over a camp-fire, after twelve hours in the saddle, — the fresh breeze fanning your cheeks, and every sense intensified by beholding the far-reaching fields blooming with flowers or waving with ripening grain?

The shadows of night are falling, and though the sun has shone through a cloudless sky the evening air is chilly. We will warm it by kindling a grand bivouac-fire, where, after supper, we will sit in solemn council, or crack jokes, or tell stories, as the whim of the hour shall lead us.

There was a time when the gray-beards of our party were youngsters and played "horse" with a wooden bit between the teeth, the reins handled by a white-haired schoolmate. How we trotted, cantered, reared, pranced, backed, and then rushed furiously on, making the little old hand-cart rattle over the stones! It was long ago, but we have not forgotten it, and to-night we will be boys once more.

Yonder by the roadside lies a fallen oak, a monarch of the forest, broken down by the wind, —

by the same tempest that levelled our tents. It shall blaze to-night. We will sit in its cheerful light. It would be ignoble to hack it to pieces and bring it into camp an armful at a time; we will drag it bodily, lop off the limbs and pile them high upon the trunk, touch a match to the withered leaves, and warm the chilly air.

"All hands to the harness!" It is a royal team. How could it be otherwise with the Ex-Governor of the Green Mountain State for leader, matched with our Judge, who, for sixteen years, honored the judiciary of Maine, with three members of Congress past and present, a doctor of divinity and another of medicine, — all in harness? We have a strong cart-rope of the best Manilla hemp, which has served us many a turn in pulling our wagons through the sloughs, and which is brought once more into service. A few strokes of the axe provide us with levers which serve for yokes. We pair off, two and two, and take our places in the team.

"Are you all ready? Now for it!" It is the voice of our leader.

"Gee up! Whoa! Whoa! Hip! Hurrah! Now she goes!"

We shout and sing, and feel an ecstatic thrill running all over us, from the tips of our fingers down into our boots!

What a deal of power there is in a yell! The

teamster screams to his horses; the plough-boy makes himself hoarse by shouting to his oxen; the fireman feels that he is doing good service when he goes tearing down the street yelling with all his might. He never would put out the fire if he could n't yell. A hurrah elected General Harrison President of the United States, and it has won many a political battle-field. A hurrah starts the old oak from its bed. See the Executive as he sets his compact shoulders to the work, making the lever bend before him. Notice the tall form of the Judge bowing in the traces! If the rope does not break, the log is bound to come.

The two are good at pulling. They have shown their power by dragging one of the greatest enterprises of modern times over obstacles that would have discouraged men of weaker nerve. The public never will know of the hard work performed by them in starting the Northern Pacific Railroad, — how they have raised it from obscurity, from obloquy, notwithstanding opposition and prejudice. The time will come when the public will look upon the enterprise in its true light. When the road is opened from Lake Superior westward, when the traveller finds on every hand a country of surpassing richness, a climate in the Northwest as mild as that of Pennsylvania, when he sees the numberless attractions and exhaustless resources of the land, then, and not till then, will the labors of Governor Smith and his associates in carrying on this work be appreciated.

To-night they enter with all the zest of youth into the project of building a camp-fire, and tug at the rope with the enthusiasm of boyhood.

It is a strong team. Our doctor of divinity, whether in the pulpit or on the prairie, pulls with "a forty parson power," to use Byron's simile. And our M. D., whether he has hold of a gnarled oak or the stump of a molar in the mouth of a pretty young lady, is certain to master it.

A member of Congress "made believe pull," as we used to say in our boyhood, but complacently smoked his pipe the while; the correspondent tipped a wink at the smoker, seized hold of a lever, shouted and yelled as if laying out all his strength, and pulled — about two pounds! But *we* dragged it in amid the hurrahs of the teamsters, wiped the sweat from our brows, and then through the evening sat round the blazing log, and made the air ring with our merry laughter. So we rubbed out the growing wrinkles, smoothed the lines of care, and turned back the shadow creeping up the dial.

A STRONG TEAM

CHAPTER VII.

IN THE FOREST.

IN preceding chapters the characteristics of the country west of the Mississippi have been set forth; but many a man seeking a new home would be lonely upon the prairies. The lumberman of Maine, who was born in the forest, who in childhood listened to the sweet but mournful music of the ever-sighing pines, would be homesick away from the grand old woods. The trees are his friends. The open country would be a solitude, but in the depths of the forest he would ever find congenial company. There the oaks, the elms, and maples reach out their arms lovingly above him, sheltering him alike from winter's blasts and summer's heats. Even though he may have no poetry in his soul, the woods will have a charm for him, for there he finds a harvest already grown and waiting to be gathered, as truly as if it were so many acres of ripened wheat.

It is not difficult to pick out the "Down-Easters" in Minnesota. When I hear a man talk about "stumpage" and "thousands of feet," I know that he is from the Moosehead region, or has been in a lumber camp on the Chesuncook. He has eaten pork and beans, and slept on hemlock boughs on the banks of the Madawaska. When he cocks his head on one side and squints up a pine-tree, I know that he has Blodget's Table in his brain, and can tell the exact amount of clear and merchantable lumber which the tree will yield. His paradise is in the forest, and there alone.

The region east of the Mississippi and around its head-waters is the Eden of lumbermen.

The traveller who starts from St. Paul and travels westward will find a prairie country; but if he travels eastward, or toward the northeast, he will find himself in the woods, where tall pines and spruces and oaks and maples rear their gigantic trunks. It is not all forest, for here and there we see "openings" where the sunlight falls on pleasant meadows; but speaking in general terms, the entire country east of the Mississippi, in Minnesota and northern Wisconsin, and in that portion of Michigan lying between Lake Superior and Lake Michigan, is the place for the lumberman.

The soil is sandy, and the geologist will see satisfactory traces of the drift period, when a great flood of waters set southward, bringing granite bowlders, pebbles, and stones from the country lying between Hudson Bay and Lake Superior.

The forest growth affects the climate. There is more snow and rain east of the Mississippi than west of it. The temperature in winter on Lake

Superior is milder than at St. Paul, but there is more moisture in the air. The climate at Duluth or Superior City during the winter does not vary much from that of Chicago. Notwithstanding the difference of latitude, the isothermal line of mean temperature for the year runs from the lower end of Lake Michigan to the western end of Lake Superior. Probably more snow falls in Minnesota than around Chicago, for in all forest regions in northern latitudes there is usually a heavier rain and snow fall than in open countries. The time will probably come when the rain-fall of eastern Minnesota and northern Michigan will be less than it is now. When the lumbermen have swept away the forests, the sun will dry up the moisture, there will be less rain east of the Mississippi, while the probabilities are that it will be increased westward over all the prairie region. Orchards, groves, corn-fields, wheat-fields, clover-lands, — all will appear with the advance of civilization. They will receive more moisture from the surrounding air than the prairie grasses do at the present time. Everybody knows that the hand of man is powerful enough to change climate, — to increase the rain-fall here, to diminish it there; to lower the temperature, or to raise it.

The Ohio River is dwindling in size because the forests of Ohio and Pennsylvania are disappearing.

Palestine, Syria, and Greece, although they have supported dense populations, are barren to-day because the trees have been cut down. If this were an essay on the power of man over nature, instead of the writing out of a few notes on the Northwest, I might go on and give abundant data; but I allude to it incidentally in connection with the climate, which fifty years hence will not in all probability be the same that it is to-day.

Having in preceding pages taken a survey of the magnificent farming region beyond the Mississippi, it remains for us to take a look at the country between the Mississippi and Lake Superior.

Leaving our camp equipage and the horses that had borne us over the prairies, bidding good by to our many friends in Minneapolis and St. Paul, we started from the last-named city for a trip of a hundred and fifty miles through the woods. The first fifty miles was accomplished by rail, through a country partially settled. Upon the train were several ladies and gentlemen on their way to White Bear Lake, not the White Bear of the West, but a lovely sheet of water ten miles north of St. Paul. It is but a few years since Wabashaw and his dusky ancestors trolled their lines by day and speared pickerel and pike by torchlight at night upon its placid bosom, but now it is the favorite resort of picnic-parties from St. Paul. Here and there along the shores are low grass-grown monuments, raised by the Chippewas when they were a powerful nation among the Red Men.

> "But now the wheat is green and high
> On clods that hid the warrior's breast,
> And scattered in the furrows lie
> The weapons of his rest."

The lake is six miles long and dotted with islands. It was a general gathering-place of the Indians, as it is now of the people of the surrounding country. Its curving shores and pebbly beaches, bordered by a magnificent forest, present a charming and peaceful picture.

We are accompanied on our trip by the President of the Lake Superior and Mississippi Railroad, and other gentlemen connected with the railroads of the Northwest. At Wyoming we leave our friends, bid good by to the locomotive, and say how do you do to a bright new mud-wagon! It is set on thorough-braces, with a canvas top. There are seats for nine inside and one with the driver outside. Carpet-bags and valises are stowed under the seats. We have no extra luggage, but are in light staging order.

We are bound for Superior and Duluth.

"You will have a sweet time getting there," is the remark of a mud-bespattered man sitting on a pile of lumber by the roadside. He has just come through on foot with a dozen men, who have thrown down the shovel to take up the sickle, or rather to follow the reaper during harvest.

What he means by our having a sweet time we do not quite comprehend.

"You will find the road baddish in spots," says another.

A German, with bushy beard and uncombed hair, barefooted, and carrying his boots in his hands, exclaims, "It ish von tam tirty travel all the time!"

We understand him. With a crack of the whip we roll away, our horses on the trot, passing cleared fields, where cattle are up to their knees in clover, past wheat-fields ready for the reaper, reaching at noon our halting-place for dinner.

Whenever you find a farm-house anywhere out West where there are delicious apple-pies, or anything especially nice in the pastry line, on the table, you may be pretty sure that the hostess came from Maine; at least, such has been my experience. I remember calling at a house in central Missouri during the war, and, instead of having the standard dish of the Southwest "hog and hominy," obtaining a luxurious dinner, finishing off with apple-pie, the pastry moulded by fair hands that were trained to housework on the banks of the Penobscot. Last year I found a lady from Maine among the Sierra Nevadas; I was confident that she was from the Pine-Tree State the moment I saw her pies; for somehow the daughters of Down East have the knack of making pastry that would delight an epicure. And now in Minnesota we sit down to a substantial dinner topped off, rounded, and made complete by a piece of Maine apple-pie.

The daughters of New Hampshire and of Vermont may possibly make just as good cooks, but it has so happened that we have fallen in with housewives from Maine when our appetite was sharpened for something good.

Our dinner is at the house of a farmer who came to Minnesota from the Kennebec. He knew how to swing an axe, and the oaks and maples have fallen before his sturdy strokes; the plough and harrow and stump-puller have been at work, and now we look out upon wheat-fields and acres of waving corn, inhale the fragrance of white clover, and hear the humming of the bees. We see at a glance the capabilities of the forest region of Minnesota. We understand it just as well as if we were to read all the works extant on soil, climatology, natural productions, etc. Here, as well as westward of the Mississippi, wheat, corn, potatoes, clover, and timothy can be successfully and profitably cultivated.

"I raised thirty-five bushels of wheat to the acre last year, and I guess I shall have that this year," said the owner of the farm.

This well-to-do farmer and his wife came here without capital, or rather with capital arms and strong hearts, to rear a home, and here it is: a neat farm-house of two stories; a carpet on the floor, a sofa, a rocking-chair, pictures on the walls; a large barn; granary well filled, — a comfortable home with a bright future before them.

When the timber has disappeared from eastern Minnesota, the land will produce luxuriantly. The country will not be settled quite as rapidly here as west of the Mississippi; but it is not to be forever a wilderness. The time will come when along every stream there will be heard the buzzing of saws, the whirring of mill-stones, and the click and clatter of machinery. This vast area of timber will invite every kind of manufacturing, and the same elements which have contributed so largely to build up the Eastern States — the manufacturing and industrial — will here aid in building up one of the strongest communities of our future republic.

Clearings here and there, cabins by the roadside, bark wigwams which have sheltered wandering Ojibwas, and a reach of magnificent forest, are the features of the country through which we ride this glorious afternoon, with the sunlight glimmering among the trees, till suddenly we come upon Chengwatona.

It is a small village on Snake River, with a

hotel, half a dozen houses, and a saw-mill where pine logs are going up an incline from the pond at one end, and coming out in the shape of bright new lumber at the other.

The dam at Chengwatona has flooded an immense area, and looking toward the descending sun we behold a forest in decay. The trees are leafless, and the dead trunks rising from the water, robbed of all their beauty, present an indescribable scene of desolation when contrasted with the luxuriance of the living forest through which we have passed.

With a fresh team we move on, finding mud "spots" now and then. We remember the remarks of the fellows at the railroad. We dive into holes, the forward wheels going down *kerchug*, sending bucketsful of muddy water upward to the roof of the wagon and forward upon the horses; jounce over corduroy which sets our teeth to chattering; then come upon a series of hollows through which we ride as in a jolly-boat on the waves of the sea. The wagon is ballasted by two members of Congress on the back seat, and by our rotund physician and the Vice-President of the Northern Pacific on the middle seat. The President is outside with the driver, on the lookout for breakers, while the rest of us, like passengers on shipboard, stowed beneath the hatches, must take whatever comes. The members of Congress bob up and down like electric pith-balls between the negative and positive poles of a galvanic battery, — only that the positive is the prevailing force! When the forward wheels go down to the hub, they go up; and then, as they descend, the seat, by some unaccountable process, comes up, meets them half-way, — and with such a bump!

Then we who are shaking our sides with laughter on the front seat, congratulating ourselves, like the Pharisees, that we are not as they are, suddenly find ourselves sprawling on the floor. When we regain our places, the M. D. and Vice-President come forward with a rush and embrace us fraternally. We get our legs so mixed up with our neighbors' that we can hardly tell whether our feet belong to ourselves or to somebody else! The light weights of the party are knocked about like shuttlecocks, while the solid ones roll like those ridiculous, round-bottomed, grinning images that we see in the toy-shops! I find myself going up and down after the manner of Sancho Panza when tossed in a blanket.

Our dinners are well settled when we reach Grindstone, — our stopping-place for the night. The town is located on Grindstone Creek, and consists of a log-house and stable, surrounded by burnt timber.

Half a dozen men who have footed it from Duluth are nursing their sore feet in one of the three rooms on the ground-floor. The furniture of the apartment consists of a cast-iron stove in the centre and three rough benches against the walls, which are papered with pictorial newspapers.

The occupants are discussing the future prospects of Duluth.

"It is a right smart chance of a place," says a tall, thin-faced, long-nosed man stretched in one corner. We know by the utterance of that one sentence that he is from southern Illinois.

"They have got their *i*-deas pretty well up though, on real estate, for a town that is only a yearlin'," says another, who, by his accent of the *i*, has shown that he too is a Western man.

An Amazon in stature, with a round red face, hurries up a supper of pork and fried eggs; and then we who are going northward, and they who are travelling southward, — sixteen of us, all told, — creep up the narrow stairway to the unfinished garret, and go to bed, with our noses close to the rafters and long shingles, through the crevices of which we look out and behold the stars marching in grand procession across the midnight sky.

It is glorious to lie there and feel the *tire* and weariness go out of us; to look into the "eternities of space," as Carlyle says of the vault of heaven. But our profound thoughts upon the measureless empyrean are brought down to sublunary things by four of the sleepers who engage in a snoring contest. The race is so close, neck and neck, or rather nose and nose, that it is impossible to decide whether the deep sonorous — not to say *snorous?* — bass of the big fellow by the window, or the sharp, piercing, energetic snorts of the thin-faced, lantern-jawed, long-nosed man from southern Illinois, is entitled to the trumpet or horn, or whatever may be appropriate to signalize such championship. Either of them would have been a power in the grand chorus of the Coliseum Jubilee, and both together would be equal to the big organ!

We are off early in the morning, feeling a little sore in spots. The first thump extorts a sudden oh! from a member of Congress, but we are philosophic, and accommodate ourselves to circumstances, tell stories between the bumpings, and make the grand old forest ring with our laughter. It is glorious to get away from the town, and out into the woods, where you can shout and sing and let yourself out without regard to what folks will say! The fountain of perennial youth is in the forest, — never in the city. Its healing, beautifying, and restoring waters do not run through aqueducts; they are never pumped up; but you must lie down upon the mossy bank beneath old trees and drink from the crystal stream to obtain them.

We quench our thirst from gurgling brooks, pick

berries by the roadside, walk ahead of the lumbering stage, and enjoy the solitude of the interminable forest.

Eighteen miles of travel brings us to Kettle River Crossing, where we sit down to a dinner of blackberries and milk, bread and butter, and blackberry-pie, in a clean little cottage, with pictures on the walls, books on a shelf, a snow-white cloth on the table, and a trim little woman waiting upon us.

"May I ask where you are from?"

"Manchester, New Hampshire."

It was Lord Morpeth or the Duke of Argyle, I have forgotten which, who said that New England looked as if it had just been taken out of a bandbox; so with this one-storied log-house and everything around it. We had sour-krout at Grindstone, but have blackberries here; and that is just the difference between Dutchland and New England, whether you seek for them on the Atlantic slope or in the heart of the continent.

Space is wanting to tell of all the incidents of a three days' forest ride, — how we trolled for pickerel on a little lake, seated in a birch-bark canoe, and hauled them in hand over hand, — bouncing fellows that furnished us a delicious breakfast; how we laughed and told stories, never minding the bumping and thumping of the wagon, and came out strong, like Mark Tapley, every one of us; how we gazed upon the towering pines and sturdy oaks, and beheld the gloom settling over nature when the great eclipse occurred; and how, just as night was coming on, we entered Superior, and saw a horned owl sitting on the ridge-pole of a deserted house in the outskirts of the town, surveying the desolate scene in the twilight, — looking out upon the cemetery, the tenantless houses, and the blinking lights in the windows.

Superior has been, and still is, a city of the Future, rather than of the Present. It was laid out before the war on a magnificent scale by a party of Southerners, among whom was John C. Breckenridge, who is still a large owner in corner lots.

It has a fine situation at the southwestern corner of the lake, on a broad, level plateau, with a densely timbered country behind it. The St. Louis River, which rises in northern Minnesota, and which comes tumbling over a series of cascades formed by the high land between Lake Superior and the Mississippi, spreads itself out into a shallow bay in front of the town, and reaches the lake over a sand-bar.

Government has been erecting breakwaters to control the current of the river, with the expectation of deepening the channel, which has about nine feet of water; but thus far the improvements have not accomplished the desired end. The bar is a great impediment to navigation, and its existence has had a blighting effect on the once fair prospects of Superior City. Dredges are employed to deepen the channel, but those thus far used are small, and not much has been accomplished. The citizens of Superior are confident that with a liberal appropriation from government the channel can be deepened, and that, when once cleared out, it can be kept clear at a small expense.

Superior has suffered severely from the reaction which followed the flush times in 1857. A large amount of money was expended in improvements, — grading streets, opening roads, building piers, and erecting houses. Then the war came on, and all industry was paralyzed. The Southern proprietors were in rebellion. The growth of the place, which had been considerable, came to a sudden stand-still.

The situation of the town, while it is fortunate in some respects, is unfortunate in others. It is in Wisconsin, while the point which reaches across the head of the lake is in Minnesota. The last-named State wanted a port on the lake in its own dominion, and so Duluth has sprung into existence as the rival of its older neighbor.

The St. Paul and Superior Railroad, having its terminus at Duluth, lies wholly within the State of Minnesota, and comes just near enough to Superior to tantalize and vex the good people of that place.

But the citizens of that town have good pluck. I do not know what motto they have adopted for their great corporate seal, but *Nil Desperandum* would best set forth their hopefulness and determination. They are confident that Superior is yet to be the queen city of the lake, and are determined to have railway communication with the Mississippi by building a branch line to the St. Paul and Superior Road.

Our party is kindly and hospitably entertained by the people of the place, and to those who think of the town as being so far northwest that it is beyond civilization, I have only to say that there are few drawing-rooms in the East where more agreeable company can be found than that which we find in one of the parlors of Superior; few places where the sonatas of Beethoven and Mendelssohn can be more exquisitely rendered upon the pianoforte, by a lady who bakes her own bread and cares for her family without the aid of a servant.

It is the glory of our civilization that it adapts itself to all the circumstances of life. I have no doubt that if Minnie, or Winnie, or Georgiana, or almost any of the pale, attenuated young ladies who are now frittering away their time in studying the last style of *paniers*, or thrumming the piano, or reading the last vapid novel, were to have their lot cast in the West,—on the frontiers of civilization,—where they would be *compelled* to do something for themselves or those around them, that they would manfully and *womanfully* accept the situation, be far happier than they now are, and worth more to themselves and to the world.

I dare say that nine out of every ten young men selling dry-goods in retail stores in Boston and elsewhere have high hopes for the future. They are going to do something by and by. When they get on a little farther they will show us what they can accomplish. But the chances are that they will never get that little farther on. The tide is against them. One thing we are liable to forget; we measure ourselves by what we are going to do, whereas the world estimates us by what we have already done. How any young man of spirit can settle himself down to earning a bare existence, when all this vast region of the Northwest, with its boundless undeveloped resources before him, is inviting him on, is one of the unexplained mysteries of life. They will be Nobodies where they are; they can be Somebodies in building up a new society. The young man who has measured off ribbon several years, as thousands have who are doing no better to-day than they did five years ago, in all probability will be no farther along, except in years, five years hence than he is now.

CHAPTER VIII.

DULUTH.

EMBARKING at a pier, and steering north-west, we pass up the bay, with the long, narrow, natural breakwater, Minnesota Point, on our right hand, and the level plateau of the main-land, with a heavy forest growth, on our left. Before us, on the sloping hillside of the northern shore, lies the rapidly rising town of Duluth, unheard of twelve months ago, but now, to use a Western term, "a right smart chance of a place."

One hundred and ninety years ago Duluth, a French explorer, was coasting along these shores, and sailing up this bay over which we are gliding. He was the first European to reach the head of the lake. He crossed the country to the Upper Mississippi, descended it to St. Paul, where he met Father Hennipen, who had been held in captivity by the Indians.

It is suitable that so intrepid an explorer should be held in remembrance, and the founders of the new town have done wisely in naming it for him, instead of calling it Washington or Jackson, or adding another "ville" to the thousands now so perplexing to post-office clerks.

The new city of the Northwest is sheltered from northerly winds by the high lands behind it. The St. Louis River, a stream as large as the Merrimac, after its turbulent course down the rocky rapids, with a descent altogether of five hundred feet, flows peacefully past the town into the Bay of Superior. The river and lake together have thrown up the long and narrow strip of land called Minnesota Point, reaching nearly across the head of the lake, and behind which lies the bay. It is as if the Titans had thrown up a wide railway embankment, or had tried their hand at filling up the lake. The bay is shallow, but the men who projected the city of Duluth are in no wise daunted by that fact. They have planned to make a harbor by building a mole out into the lake fifteen hundred or two thousand feet. It is to extend from the northern shore far enough to give good anchorage and protection to vessels and steamers.

The work to be done is in many respects similar to what has been accomplished at both ends of the Suez Canal. When M. Lesseps set about the construction of that magnificent enterprise, he found no harbor on the Mediterranean side, but only a low sandy shore, against which the waves, driven by the prevailing western winds, were always breaking.

The shore was a narrow strip of sand, behind which lay a shallow lagoon called Lake Menzaleh.

There was no granite or solid material of any description at hand for the construction of a breakwater. Undaunted by the difficulties, he commenced the manufacture of blocks of stone on the beach, mixing hydraulic lime brought from France with the sand of the shore, and moistening it with salt water. He erected powerful hydraulic presses and worked them by steam. After the blocks, which weighed twenty tons each, had dried three months, they were taken out on barges and tumbled into the ocean in the line of the moles, one of which was 8,178 feet, nearly a mile and a half, in length; the other 5,000 feet, enclosing an area of about five hundred acres. More than 100,000 blocks of manufactured stone were required to complete these two walls. They were not laid in cement, for it has been found that a rubble wall is better than finished masonry to resist the action of the waves. Having completed the walls, dredges were set to work, and the area has been deepened enough to enable the largest vessels navigating the Mediterranean to find safe anchorage.

These breakwaters were required for the outer harbor, but an inner basin was needed. To obtain it, M. Lesseps cut a channel through the low ridge of sand to Lake Menzaleh, where the water upon an average was four feet deep. A large area has been dredged in the lake, and docks constructed, and now the commerce of the world between the Orient and the Occident passes through the basin of Port Said.

The Suez Canal, the construction of a large harbor on the sand-beach of the Mediterranean, and another of equal capacity on the Red Sea, is one of the wonders of modern times, — a triumph of engineering skill and of the indomitable will of one energetic man.

The people of Duluth will not be under the necessity of manufacturing the material for the breakwater, for along the northern shore there is an abundant supply of granite which can be easily quarried. It is proposed to make an inner harbor by digging a canal across Minnesota Point and excavating the shallows.

The difficulties to be overcome at Duluth bear slight comparison with those already surmounted on the Mediterranean. The commercial men of Chicago contemplate the fencing in of a few hundred acres of Lake Michigan; and there is no reason to doubt that a like thing can be done at the western end of Lake Superior.

Two years ago Duluth was a forest; but in this month of May, 1870, it has two thousand inhabitants, with the prospect of doubling its population within a twelvemonth. The woodman's axe is ringing on the hills, and the trees are falling beneath his sturdy strokes. From morning till night we hear the joiner's plane and the click of the mason's trowel. You may find excellent accommodation in a large hotel, erected at a cost of forty thousand dollars. We may purchase the products of all climes in the stores, — sugar from the West Indies, coffee from Java, tea from China, or silks from the looms of France.

The printing-press is here issuing the Duluth Minnesotian, a sprightly sheet that looks sharply after the interests of this growing town.

Musical as the ripples upon the pebbly shore of the lake are the voices of the children reciting their lessons in yonder school-house. I am borne back to boyhood days, — to the old school-house, with its hard benches, where I studied, played, caught flies, was cheated swapping jack-knives, and got a licking besides! Glorious days they were for all that!

Presbyterian and Episcopal churches are already organized, also an Historical Society. During the last winter a course of lectures was sustained.

The stumps are yet to be seen in the streets, but such is the beginning of a town which may yet become one of the great commercial cities of the interior.

A meteorological record kept at Superior since 1855 shows that the average period of navigation has been two hundred and sixteen days, which is fully as long as the season at Chicago.

Year.	Opening.	Close.	No. of Days.
1855	April 15	December 6	235
1856	" 16	November 22	220
1857	May 27	" 20	177
1858	March 20	" 22	247
1859	May 25	" 9	164
1860	April 7	December 4	238
1861	June 12	" 12	184
1862	April 28	" 16	233
1863	May 10	" 7	212
1864	April 23	" 1	222
1865	" 22	" 5	227
1866	May 5	" 10	220
1867	April 19	" 1	225

Steaming up the river several miles to the foot of the first rapids, and landing on the northern shore, climbing up a wet and slippery bank of red clay we are on the line of the railroad, upon which several hundred men are employed.

Grades of fifty feet to the mile are necessary from the lake up to the falls of the St. Louis, but the tonnage of the road will be largely eastward, down the grade, instead of westward.

The road will be about a hundred and forty miles in length, connecting the lake with the network of railroads centring at St. Paul. It is liberally endowed, having in all 1,630,000 acres of land heavily timbered with pine, butternut, white oak, sugar-maple, ash, and other woods.

There is no doubt that this line of road will do an immense amount of business. Such is the estimation in which it is held by the moneyed men of Philadelphia, that Mr. Jay Cooke obtained the entire amount of money necessary to construct it in four days! The bonds, I believe, were not put upon the market in the usual manner, by advertising, but were taken at once by men who wanted them for investment.

A single glance at the map must be sufficient to convince any intelligent observer of the value of such a franchise. The wheat of Minnesota, to reach Chicago now, must be taken by steamers to La Crosse or Prairie du Chien, and thence transported by rail across Wisconsin, but when this road is put in operation, the products of Minnesota, gathered at St. Paul or Minneapolis, will seek this new outlet.

Think of the scene of activity there will be along the line, not only of this road, but of the Northern Pacific, when the two are completed to the lake, of an almost continuous train of cars, of elevators pouring grain from cars to ships and steamers. Think of the fleet that will soon whiten this great inland sea, bearing the products of the immense wheat-field eastward to the Atlantic cities, and bringing back the industries of the Eastern States!

It is only when I sit down to think of the future, to measure it by the advancement already made, that I can comprehend anything of the coming greatness of the Northwest, — 20,000,000 bushels of wheat this year; 500,000 inhabitants in the State, yet scarcely a hundredth part of the area under cultivation. What will be the product ten years hence, when the population will reach 1,500,000? What will it be twenty years hence? How shall we obtain any conception of the business to be done on these railways when Dakota, Montana, Washington, and Oregon, and all the vast region of the Assinniboine and the Saskatchawan, pour their products to the nearest water-carriage eastward? We are already beyond our depth, and are utterly unable to comprehend the probable development.

The men who are building this railroad from St. Paul to Duluth have not failed to recognize this one fact, that by water Duluth is as near as Chicago to the Atlantic cities. Wheat and flour can be transported as cheaply from Duluth to Buffalo or Ogdensburg as from the southern end of Lake Michigan, while the distance from St. Paul to Lake Superior is only one hundred and forty miles against four hundred and eighty to Chicago. We may conclude that the wheat of Minnesota can be carried fifteen or twenty cents a bushel cheaper by Duluth than by Lake Michigan, — a saving to the Eastern consumer of almost a dollar on each barrel of flour. Twenty cents on a bushel saved will add at least four dollars to the yearly product of an acre of land.

The difference in freight on articles manufactured in the East and shipped to Minnesota will be still more marked, for grain in bulk is taken at low rates, while manufactured goods pay first-class. The completion of this railway will be a great blessing to the people of New England and of all the East, as well as to those of the Northwest. Anything that abridges distance and cheapens carriage is so much absolute gain. I do not think that there is any public enterprise in the country that promises to produce more important results than the opening of this railway.

An elevator company has been organized by several gentlemen in Boston and Philadelphia, and the necessary buildings are now going up. The wheat will be taken directly from the cars into the elevator, and discharged into the fleet of propellers running to Cleveland, Buffalo, and Ogdensburg, already arranged for this Lake Superior trade.

The region around the western end of the Lake has resources for the development of a varied industry. The wooded section extends from Central Wisconsin westward to the Leaf Hills beyond the Mississippi, and northward to Lake Winnipeg. This is to be the lumbering region of the Northwest, for the manufacture of all agricultural implements, — reapers, mowers, harvesters, ploughs, drills, seed-sowers, wagons, carriages, carts, and furniture,—besides furnishing lumber for fencing, for railroad and building purposes.

Upon the St. Louis River there is exhaustless water-power, — a descent of five hundred feet, with a stream always pouring an abundant flood. Its source is among the lakes of northern Minnesota, which, being filled to overflowing by the rains of spring and early summer, become great reservoirs. With such a supply of water there is no locality more favorably situated for the manufacture of every variety of domestic articles. Undoubtedly the water-power will be largely employed for flouring-mills. The climate is admirably adapted to the grinding of grain. The falls being so near the lake, there will be cheap transportation eastward to Buffalo, Cleveland, Philadelphia, New York, and Boston, while westward are the prairies, easily reached by the railroads.

The geological formation on the north side of Lake Superior is granite, but as we follow up the St. Louis River we come upon a ridge of slate. It forms the backbone of the divide between the lake and the Mississippi River.

A quarry has been opened from which slates of a quality not inferior to those of Vermont are obtained, and so far as we know it is the only quarry in the Northwest. It is almost invaluable, for Nebraska, Kansas, Iowa, western Minnesota, and Dakota have very little wood. Shingles are costly, but here is abundant material to cover the roofs of the millions of houses that are yet to rise upon the prairies.

This slate formation is thus referred to by Thomas Clark, State Geologist, in his Report to the Governor of Minnesota, dated December, 1864 (pp. 29, 30): —

"These slates are found in all degrees of character, from the common indurated argillaceous fissile to the highly metamorphosed and even trappous type. The working of these slates demands the attention of builders; their real value is economically of more importance to the prairie and sparsely timbered valley of the Mississippi than any other deposit in the State's possession on the lake. The annual draught of hundreds of millions of lumber upon the pine forests of the St. Croix and Upper Mississippi and tributaries will exhaust those regions before the close of this century. The trustees of our young Commonwealth are emphatically admonished to encourage and foster the working of these slates, and to bring them into use at the earliest time possible. A hundred square feet of dressed slates at the quarries of Vermont, New York, and Canada are worth from one and a half to two dollars; the weight ranges from four to six hundred pounds, or about four squares to the ton. A ton of this roofing may be transported from the St. Louis quarry to the Mississippi, by railway, at three dollars, and thence by river to the landings as far down as St. Louis or Cairo; but the article may be at all points in this State accessible by boats or railway, at an average cost of fifteen dollars per ton, or, at most, four dollars per square, — little, if any, more than pine shingles; the former as good for a century as the latter is for a decade. The supply of these cliffs is literally inexhaustible; if one fourth of this slate area in the St. Louis Valley proves available, — and doubtless one half will, — it will yield one thousand millions of tons.

"The demand for this slate at ten roofs to the square mile, and for forty thousand square miles, would be one million of tons, or one thousandth part of the material. The annual demand for slates in the Mississippi Valley may be reasonably estimated at one hundred thousand tons, an exportable product of two hundred thousand dollars, besides the element of a permanent income to the railways and water-craft of the State of a half-million of dollars annually."

To-day the country along the St. Louis is a wilderness. Climb the hills, and look upon the scene, and think of the coming years.

"Thou shalt look
Upon the green and rolling forest tops,
And down into the secrets of the glens
And streams, that with their bordering thickets strive
To hide their windings. Thou shalt gaze at once,

Here on white villages, and tilth and herds,
And swarming roads, and there on solitudes
That only hear the torrent, and the wind,
And eagle's shriek."

Here, through the bygone centuries, the Indians have set their nets and hooks without ever dreaming of laying their hands upon the wealth that Nature has ever in store for those who will labor for it.

A few of the original lords of the forests are here, and they are the only idlers of this region. They lounge in the streets, squat in groups under the lee of buildings, and pick animated *somethings* from their hair!

Their chief appears in an old army coat with three stars on each shoulder, indicating that he ranks as a lieutenant-general among his people. He walks with dignity, although his old black stove-pipe hat is badly squashed. The warriors follow him, wrapped in blankets, with eagle feathers stuck into their long black hair, and are as dignified as the chief. Labor! not they. Pale-faces and squaws may work, they never. Squaw-power is their highest conception of a labor-saving machine. They have fished in the leaping torrent, but never thought of its being a giant that might be put to work for their benefit.

It is evident that a great manufacturing industry must spring up in this region. At Minneapolis, St. Cloud, and here on the St. Louis, we find the three principal water-powers of the Northwest. The town of Thompson, named in honor of one of the proprietors, Mr. Edgar A. Thompson of Philadelphia, has been laid out at the falls, and being situated on the line of the railroad, and so convenient to the lake, will probably have a rapid growth. The St. Paul and Mississippi Railroad, which winds up the northern bank of the river, crosses the stream at that point, and strikes southward through the forests to St. Paul.

The road, in addition to its grant of land, has received from the city of St. Paul $ 200,000 in city bonds, and this county of St. Louis at the head of the lake has given $ 150,000 in county bonds.

The lands of this company are generally heavily timbered, — with pine, maple, ash, oak, and other woods.

The white pines of this region are almost as magnificent as those that formerly were the glory of Maine and New Hampshire. Norway pines abound. Besides transporting the lumber from its own extensive tracts and the lands of the government adjoining, it will be the thoroughfare for an immense territory drained by the Snake, Kettle, St. Louis, and St. Croix Rivers.

The lands that bear such magnificent forest-trees are excellent for agriculture. Nowhere in the East have I ever seen ranker timothy and clover than we saw on our journey from St. Paul.

The company offer favorable terms to all settlers. Men from Maine and New Hampshire are already locating along the line, and setting up saw-mills. They were lumbermen in the East, and they prefer to follow the same business in the West, rather than to speed the plough for a living. I doubt not that the chances for making money are quite as good in the timbered region as on the prairies, for the lumber will pay for the land several times over, which, when put into grain or grass, yields enormously.

CHAPTER IX.

THE MINING REGION.

THE sun was throwing his morning beams upon the tree-tops of the Apostle Islands, as our little steamer, chartered for the occasion at Superior, rounded the promontory of the main-land, turned its prow southward, and glided into the harbor of Bayfield, on the southern shore of the lake.

We had made the passage from Superior City during the night, and were on deck at daybreak to see the beauties of the islands, of which so much has been written by explorers and tourists. The scenery is not bold, but beautiful. Perhaps there is no place on the lake where more charming vistas open to the eye, or where there is such a succession of entrancing views.

The islands, eighteen in number, lie north of the promontory. They would appear as high hills, with rounded summits, crowned with a dense forest growth, if the waters were drained off; for all around, between the islands and the mainland, are deep soundings. There is no harbor on the Atlantic coast, none in the world, more accessible than Bayfield, or more securely land-locked. It may be approached during the wildest storm, no matter which way the wind is blowing. When the north-easters raise a sea as terrible as that which sometimes breaks upon Nahant, the captains of steamers and schooners on Lake Superior run for the Apostle Islands.

Bayfield is about sixty miles from Superior City, and is the first harbor where vessels can find shelter east of the head of the lake. The Apostle Islands seem to have been dumped into the lake for the benefit of the mighty tide of commerce which in the coming years is to float upon this inland sea.

"It is," said our captain, "the only first-class harbor on the lake. It can be approached in all weathers; the shores are bold, the water deep, the anchorage excellent, and the ice leaves it almost two weeks earlier in spring than the other harbors at the head of the lake."

The town of Bayfield is named for an officer of the Royal Engineers, who was employed years ago in surveying the lake. His work was well done, and till recently his charts have been relied on by the sailing-masters; but the surveys of the United States Engineers, now approaching completion, are more minute and accurate.

The few houses that make up the town are beautifully located, on the western side of the bay. Madeline Island, the largest of the group, lies immediately in front, and shelters the harbor and town from the northeast storms.

The scream of the steamer's whistle rings sharply on the morning air, — while main-land and island, harbor and forest, repeat its echoes. It wakes up all the braves, squaws, and pappooses in the wigwams and log-houses of the Chippewa reservation, and all the inhabitants of Bayfield. The sun is just making his appearance when we run alongside the pier. It is an early hour for a dozen strangers, with sharp-set appetites, to make a morning call,— more than that, to drop in thus unceremoniously upon a private citizen for breakfast.

There being no hotel in the place, we are put to this strait. Possibly old Nokomis, who is cooking breakfast in a little iron pot with a big piece knocked out of its rim, who squats on the ground and picks out the most savory morsels with her fingers, would share her meal with us, but she does not invite us to breakfast, nor do we care to make ourselves at home in the wigwam.

But there is rare hospitality awaiting us. A gentleman who lives in a large white house in the centre of the town, Captain Vaughn, though not through with his morning nap when we steam up the harbor, is wide awake in an instant.

I wonder if there is another housewife in the United States who would provide such an ample repast as that which, in an incredibly short space of time, appeared on the table, prepared by Mrs. Vaughn, — such a tender steak, mealy potatoes, nice biscuit, delicious coffee, berries and sweet milk; a table-cloth as white as the driven snow; and the hostess the picture of health, presiding at the table with charming ease and grace, not at all disturbed by such an avalanche of company at such an hour!

Where the breakfast came from, or who cooked it so quickly, is an unexplained mystery; and then there was a basketful of lunch put up by somebody for us to devour while coasting about the bay, and the hostess the while found time to talk with us, to sit down to the parlor organ and charm us with music. So much for a Bayfield lady, born in Ohio, of stanch Yankee stock.

Embarking on Captain Vaughn's little steam-yacht, we go dancing along the shores, now running near the bluffs to examine the sandstone formation like that of the Hudson, or looking up to the tall pines waving their dark green plumes, or beholding the lumbermen felling the old monarchs and dragging them with stout teams to the Bayfield saw-mills. A run of about fifteen miles brings us to the city of Ashland, situated at the head of the bay. It makes quite an imposing appearance when you are several miles distant, and upon landing you find that you have been *imposed* upon. Somebody came here years ago, laid out a town, surveyed the lots, cut out magnificent avenues through the forest, found men who believed that Ashland was to be a great city, who bought lots and built houses; but the crowd did not come; the few who came soon turned their backs upon the place, leaving all their improvements. One German family remains. Two pigs were in possession of a parlor in one deserted house, and a cow quietly chewing her cud in another.

A mile east of Ashland is Bay City, another place planned by speculators, but which probably might be purchased at a discount.

The country around Bayfield is in a primitive condition now, but the time is rapidly approaching for a change. By and by this will be a great resort for tourists and seekers after health. Nature has made it for a *sanitarium.* No mineral springs have been discovered warranted to cure all diseases, but nowhere in this Northwest has nature compounded purer air, distilled sweeter water, or painted lovelier landscapes. The time will come when the people of Chicago, Milwaukie, and other Western cities, seeking rest and recreation during the summer months, will flee to this harbor of repose. The fish are as numerous here, and as eager to bite the hook, as anywhere else on the lake, while the streams of the main-land abound with trout. By and by this old red sandstone will be transformed into elegant mansions overlooking the blue waters, and it would not be strange if commerce reared a great mart around this harbor.

The charter of the Northern Pacific Railroad extends to this point, and as the road would pass through heavily timbered lands, the company will find it for their interest to open the line, as it will also form a connecting link between the West and the iron region of Lake Superior.

But whether a city rises here, whether a railroad is constructed or not, let me say to any one who wants to pull out big trout that this is the place.

An Indian who has been trying his luck shows a string of five-pounders, caught in one of the small streams entering the bay. There is no sport like trout-fishing. Think of stealing on tiptoe along the winding stream, dropping your hook into the gurgling waters, and feeling a moment later something tugging, turning, pulling, twisting, running, now to the right, now to the left, up stream, down stream, making the thin cord spin, till your heart leaps into your throat through fear of its breaking, — fear giving place to hope, hope to triumph, when at length you land a seven-pounder on the green and mossy bank! You find such trout in the streams that empty into the lake opposite the Apostle Islands, — trout mottled with crimson and gold!

Bidding good by to our generous host and hostess we take an eastward-bound steamer in the evening for a trip down the lake, stopping for an hour or two at Ontonagon, then steaming on, rounding Keweenaw Point during the night, and reaching Marquette in the morning.

Fishing-boats are dancing on the waves, yachts scudding along the shore, tourists rambling over the rocks at our right hand, throwing their lines, pulling up big trout, steamers and schooners are lying in the harbor, and thrift, activity, and enterprise is everywhere visible.

We see an immense structure, resembling a railway bridge, built out into the harbor. It is several hundred feet in length, and twenty or more in height. A train of cars comes thundering down a grade, and out upon the bridge, while men running from car to car knock out here and there a bolt or lift a catch, and we hear a rumbling and thundering, and feel the wharf tremble beneath our feet. It is not an earthquake; they are only unloading iron ore from the cars into bins.

A man by means of machinery raises a trapdoor, and the black mass, starting with a rush, thunders once more as it plunges into the hold of a schooner. It requires but a few minutes to take in a cargo. And then, shaking out her sails, the schooner shapes her course eastward along the "Pictured Rocks" for the St. Mary's Canal, bound for Cleveland, Erie, or Chicago with her freight of crude ore to be smelted and rolled where coal is near at hand.

The town is well laid out. Although the business portion was destroyed by fire not many months ago, it has been rebuilt. There are elegant residences, churches, school-houses, and stores. Men walk the streets as if they had a little more business on hand than they could well attend to.

The men who used to frequent this region to trade with the Indians knew as early as 1830 that iron existed in the hills. But it was not till 1845, just a quarter of a century ago, that any attempt was made to test the ore. Dr. Jackson, of Boston, who visited Lake Superior in 1844, pronounced it of excellent quality. He informed Mr. Lyman Pray, of Charlestown, Mass., of its existence, and that the Indians reported a "mountain" of it not far from Marquette. Mr. Pray at once started on an exploring expedition, reached Lake Superior, obtained an Indian guide, penetrated the forest, and found the hills filled with ore.

About the same time a gentleman named Everett obtained half a ton of it, which the Indians and half-breeds carried on their backs to the Carp River, and transported it to the lake in canoes.

It was smelted, but was so different from that of Pennsylvania that the iron-masters shook their heads. Some declared that it was of no particular value, others that it could not be worked.

The Pittsburg iron-men pronounced it worthless. But Mr. Everett persevered, sent a small quantity to the Coldwater forge, where it was smelted and rolled into a bar, from which he made a knife-blade, and was convinced that the metal was superior in quality to any other deposit in the country.

The Jackson Company was at once formed for mining in the iron and copper region. The copper fever was at its height, and the company was organized with a view of working both metals if thought advisable. A forge was erected on the Carp River in 1847, making four blooms a day, each about four feet long and eight inches thick.

Another was built, in 1854, by a company from Worcester, Mass., but so small was the production that in 1856 the shipment only reached five thousand tons. The superior qualities of the metal began to be known. Other companies were formed and improvements made; railroads and docks were constructed, and the production has had a steady increase, till it has reached a high figure.

There are fourteen companies engaged in mining, — two have just commenced, while the others are well developed. The production of the twelve principal mines for the year 1868 will be seen from the following figures: —

	Tons.
Jackson,	131,707
Cleveland,	102,213
Marquette,	7,977
Lake Superior,	105,745
New York,	45,665
Lake Angeline,	27,651
Edwards,	17,360
Iron Mountain,	3,836
Washington,	35,757
New England,	8,257
Champion,	6,255
Barnum,	14,380
Total,	506,803

The increase over the previous year is between forty and fifty thousand tons. The yield for 1869 was about 650,000 tons. The entire production of all the mines up to the close of 1868 is 2,300,000 tons.

Iron mining in this region is in its infancy; and yet the value of the metal produced last year amounts to *eighteen million dollars.*

The cause for this rapid development is found in the fact that the Lake Superior ore makes the best iron in the world. Persistent efforts were made to cry it down, but those who were engaged in its production invited rigid tests.

Its tenacity, in comparison with other qualities, will be seen by the following tabular statement:—

Swedish, ...	59
English Cable bolt, ...	59
Russian, ...	76
Lake Superior, ...	89½

When this fact was made known, railroad companies began to use Lake Superior iron for the construction of locomotives, car-wheels, and axles. Boiler builders wanted it. Those who tried it were eager to obtain more, and the result is seen in the rapidly increasing demand.

The average cost of mining and delivering the ore in cars at the mines is estimated at about $ 2 per ton. It is shipped to Cleveland at a cost of $ 4.35, making $ 6.35 when laid on the dock in that city, where it is readily sold for $ 8, leaving a profit of about $ 1.65 per ton for the shipper. Perhaps, including insurance and incidentals, the profit may be reduced to about $ 1.25 per ton. It will be seen that this is a very remunerative operation.

About one hundred furnaces in Ohio and Pennsylvania use Lake Superior ore almost exclusively, while others mix it with the ores of those regions.

A large amount is smelted at Lake Superior, where charcoal is used. The forests in the vicinity of the mines are rapidly disappearing. The wide-spreading sugar-maple, the hardy yellow birch, the feathery hackmatack and evergreen hemlock are alike tumbled into the coal-pit to supply fuel for the demands of commerce.

The charcoal consumed per ton in smelting costs about eleven cents per bushel. For reducing a ton of the best ore about a hundred and ten bushels are required; for a ton of the poorest about a hundred and forty bushels, giving an average of $ 13 per ton. The cost of mining is, as has already been stated, about $ 2 per ton. To this must be added furnace-labor, interest on capital employed, insurance, freight, commission, making the total cost about $ 35 a ton. As the iron commands the highest price in the market, it will be seen that the iron companies of Lake Superior are having an enormous income.

Some men who purchased land at government price are on the high road to fortune. One man entered eighty acres of land, which now nets him *twenty-four thousand dollars per annum !*

A railroad runs due west from Marquette, gaining by steep gradients the general level of the ridge between Superior and Michigan. It is called the Marquette and Ontonagon Railroad, and will soon form an important link in the great iron highway across the continent. It is about twenty miles from Marquette to the principal mines, which are also reached by rail from Escanaba, on Green Bay, a distance of about seventy miles.

The ore is generally found in hills ranging from

one to five hundred feet above the level of the surrounding country. The elevations can hardly be called mountains; they are knolls rather. They are iron warts on Dame Nature's face. They are partially covered with earth, — the slow-forming deposits of the alluvial period.

There are five varieties of ore. The most valuable is what is called the specular hematite, which chemically is known as a pure *anhydrous sesquioxide.* This ore yields about sixty-five per cent of pure iron. It is sometimes found in conjunction with red quartz, and is then known as mixed ore.

The next in importance is a soft hematite, resembling the ores of Pennsylvania and Connecticut. It is quite porous, is more easily reduced than any other variety, and yields about fifty per cent of pure iron.

The magnetic ores are found farther west than those already described. The Michigan, Washington, Champion, and Edwards mines are all magnetic. Sometimes the magnetic and specular lie side by side, and it is a puzzle to geologists and chemists alike to account for the difference between them. As yet we are not able to understand by what subtle alchemy the change has been produced.

Another variety is called the silicious hematite, which is more difficult of reduction than the others. It varies in richness, and there is an unlimited supply.

The fifth variety is a silicious hematite found with manganese, which, when mixed with other ores, produces an excellent quality of iron. Very little of this ore has been mined as yet, and its relative value is not ascertained.

The best iron cannot be manufactured from one variety, but by mixing ores strength and ductility both are obtained. England sends to Russia and Sweden for magnetic ores to mix with those produced in Lancashire, for the manufacture of steel. The fires of Sheffield would soon go out if the manufactures in that town were dependent on English ore alone. The iron-masters there could not make steel good enough for a blacksmith's use, to say nothing of that needed for cutlery, if they were cut off from foreign magnetic ores.

Here, at Lake Superior, those necessary for the production of the best of steel lie side by side. A mixture of the hematite and magnetic gives a metal superior, in every respect, to any that England can produce.

This one fact settles the question of the future of this region. It is to become one of the great iron-marts of the world. It is to give, by and by, the supremacy to America in the production of steel.

It is already settled, by trial, that every grade of iron now in use in arts and manufactures can be produced here at Lake Superior by mixing the various ores.

The miners are a hardy set of men, rough, uncouth, but enterprising. They live in small cottages, make excellent wages, drink whiskey, and rear large families. How happens it that in all new communities there is such an abundance of children? They throng every doorway, and by every house we see them tumbling in the dirt. Nearly every woman has a child in her arms.

We cannot expect to see the refinements and luxuries of old communities in a country where the stumps have not yet been cleared from the streets, and where the spruces and hemlocks are still waving above the cottages of the settlers, but here are the elements of society. These hard-handed men are developing this region, earning a livelihood for themselves and enriching those who employ them. Towns are springing into existence. We find Ishpeming rising out of a swamp. Imagine a spruce forest standing in a bog where the trees are so thick that there is hardly room enough for the lumbermen to swing their axes, the swamp being a stagnant pool of dark-colored water covered with green slime!

An enterprising town-builder purchased this bog for a song, and has laid out a city. Here it is, — dwelling-houses and stores standing on posts driven into the mud, or resting on the stumps.

He has filled up the streets with the *débris* from the mines. Frogs croak beneath the dwellings, or sun themselves on the sills. The town is not thus growing from the swamp because there is no solid land, but because the upland has exhaustless beds of iron ore beneath, too valuable to be devoted to building purposes.

I have seen few localities so full of promise for the future, not this one little spot in the vicinity of Marquette, but the entire metallic region between Lake Superior and Lake Michigan.

Look at the locality! It is half-way across the continent. Lake Michigan laves the southern, Superior the northern shore, while the St. Lawrence furnishes water-carriage to the Atlantic. A hundred and fifty miles of rail from Bayfield will give connection with the navigable waters of the Mississippi. Through this peninsula will yet lie the shortest route between the Atlantic and Pacific. Westward are the wheat-fields of the continent, to be peopled by an industrious and thriving community. There is no point more central than this for easy transportation.

Here, just where the future millions can be easiest served, exhaustless deposits of the best ore in the world have been placed by a Divine hand for the use and welfare of the mighty race now beginning to put forth its energies on this western hemisphere.

Towns, cities, and villages are to arise amid these hills; the forests and the hills themselves are to disappear. The product, now worth seventeen millions of dollars per annum, erelong will be valued at a hundred millions.

I think of the coming years when this place will be musical with the hum of machinery; when the stillness of the summer day and the crisp air of winter will be broken by the songs of men at work amid flaming forges, or at the ringing anvil. From Marquette, and Bayfield, and Ontonagon, and Escanaba, from every harbor on these inland seas, steamers and schooners, brigs and ships, will depart freighted with ore; hither they will come, bringing the products of the farm and workshop. Heavily loaded trains will thunder over railroads, carrying to every quarter of our vast domain the metals manufactured from the mines of Lake Superior.

We have but to think of the capabilities of this region, its extent and area, the increase of population, the development of resources, the construction of railways, the growth of cities and towns; we have only to grasp the probabilities of the future, to discern the dawning commercial greatness of this section of our country.

CHAPTER X.

A FAMILIAR TALK.

"I HAVE called to have a little talk about the West, and think that I should like a farm in Minnesota or in the Red River country," said a gentleman not long since, who introduced himself as Mr. Blotter, and who said he was "clerking it."

"I want to go out West and raise stock," said another gentleman who stopped me on the street.

"Where would you advise a fellow to go who has n't much money, but who is n't afraid to work?" said a stout young man from Maine.

"I am a machinist, and want to try my luck out West," said another young man hailing from a manufacturing town in Massachusetts.

"I am manufacturing chairs, and want to know if there is a place out West where I can build up a good business," said another.

Many other gentlemen, either in person or by letter, have asked for specific information.

It is not to be expected that I can point out the exact locality suited to each individual, or with which they would be suited, but for the benefit of all concerned I give the substance of an evening's talk with Mr. Blotter.

"I want a farm, I am tired of the city," said he.

Well, sir, you can be accommodated. The United States government has several million acres of land, — at least 30,000,000 in Minnesota, to say nothing of Dakota and the region beyond, — and you can help yourself to a farm out of any unoccupied territory. The Homestead Law of 1862 gives a hundred and sixty acres, free of cost, to actual settlers, whether foreign or native, male or female, over twenty-one years old, or to minors having served fourteen days in the army. Foreigners must declare their intention to become citizens. Under the present Pre-emption Law settlers often live on their claims many years before they are called on to pay the $ 1.25 per acre, — the land in the mean time having risen to $ 10 or $ 12 per acre. A recent decision gives single women the right to pre-empt. Five years' residence on the land is required by the Homestead Law, and it is not liable to any debts contracted before the issuing of the patent.

The State of Minnesota has a liberal law relative to the exemption of real estate from execution. A homestead of eighty acres, or one lot and house, is exempt; also, five hundred dollars' worth of furniture, besides tools, bed and bedding, sewing-machine, three cows, ten hogs, twenty sheep, a span of horses, or one horse and one yoke of oxen, twelve months' provisions for family and stock, one wagon, two ploughs, tools of a mechanic, library of a professional man, five hundred dollars' worth of stock if a trader, and various other articles.

You will find several railroad companies ready to sell you eighty, or a hundred and sixty, or six hundred and forty acres in a body, at reasonable rates, giving you accommodating terms.

"Would you take a homestead from government, or would you buy lands along the line of a railroad?"

That is for you to say. If you take a homestead it will necessarily be beyond the ten-mile limit of the land granted to the road, where the advance in value will not keep pace with lands nearer the line. You will find government lands near some of the railroads, which you can purchase for $ 2.50 per acre, cash down. The railroad companies will charge you from $ 2 to $ 10, according to location, but will give you time for payment.

"What are their terms?"

The St. Paul and Pacific Railroad, the main line of which is to be completed to the Red River this year, and which owns the branch line running from St. Paul up the east bank of the Mississippi to St. Cloud, have a million acres of prairie, meadow, and timber lands which they will sell in tracts of forty acres or more, and make the terms easy. Suppose you were to buy eighty acres at $ 8 per acre, that would give you a snug farm for $ 640. If you can pay cash down, they will make it $7 per acre,—$80 saved at the outset; but if you have only a few dollars in your pocket they will let you pay a year's interest at seven per cent to begin with, and the principal and interest in ten annual payments. The figures would then run in this way:—

Eighty acres at $8 per acre, ... $640.

	Interest.	Principal.	Total.
1st year,	$44.80		
2d "	40.32	$64.00	$104.32
3d "	35.84	64.00	99.84
4th "	31.36	64.00	95.36
5th "	26.88	64.00	90.88
6th "	22.40	64.00	86.40
7th "	17.92	64.00	81.92
8th "	13.44	64.00	77.44
9th "	8.96	64.00	72.96
10th "	4.48	64.00	68.48
11th "		64.00	64.00

"The second year will be the hardest," said Mr. Blotter, "for I shall have to fence my farm, build a cabin, and purchase stock and tools. Is there fencing material near?"

That depends upon where you locate. If you are near the line of the railway, you can have it brought by cars. If you locate near the "Big Woods" on the main line west of Minneapolis, you will have timber near at hand. Numerous saw-mills are being erected, some driven by water and others by steam. The timbered lands of the company are already held at high rates,— from $7 to $10 per acre. The country beyond the "Big Woods" is all prairie, with no timber except a few trees along the streams. It is filling up so rapidly with settlers that wood-lands are in great demand, for when cleared they are just as valuable as the prairie for farming purposes.

Many settlers who took up homesteads before the railroad was surveyed now find themselves in good circumstances, especially if they are near a station. In many places near towns, land which a year ago could have been had for $2.50 per acre is worth $20 to-day.

"Is the land in the Mississippi Valley above St. Paul any better than that of the prairies?"

Perhaps you have a mistaken idea in regard to the Mississippi Valley. There are no bottom-lands on the Upper Mississippi. The prairie borders upon the river. You will find the land on the east side better adapted to grazing than for raising wheat. The company do not hold their lands along the branch at so high a figure as on the main line. Some of my Minnesota friends say that stock-growing on the light lands east of the Mississippi is quite as profitable as raising wheat. Cattle, sheep, and horses transport themselves to market, but you must draw your grain.

If you are going into stock-raising, you can afford to be at a greater distance from a railroad station than the man who raises wheat. It would undoubtedly be for the interest of the company to sell you their outlying lands along the branch line at a low figure, for it would enhance the value of those nearer the road. You will find St. Cloud and Anoka thriving places, which, with St. Paul and Minneapolis, will give a good home demand for beef and mutton, to say nothing of the facilities for reaching Eastern markets by the railroads and lakes.

"Do the people of Minnesota use fertilizers?"

No; they allow the manure to accumulate around their stables, or else dump it into the river to get rid of it!

They sow wheat on the same field year after year, and return nothing to the ground. They even burn the straw, and there can be but one result coming from such a process, — exhaustion of the soil, — poor, worn-out farms by and by.

The farmers of the West are cruel towards Mother Earth. She freely bestows her riches, and then, not satisfied with her gifts, they plunder her. Men everywhere are shouting for an eight-hour law; they must have rest, time for recreation and improvement of body and mind; but they give the soil no time for recuperation. Men expect to be paid for their labors, but they make no payment to the kind mother who feeds them; they make her work and live on nothing. Farming, as now carried on in the West and Northwest, is downright robbery and plunder, and nothing else. If the present exhaustive system is kept up, the time will come when the wheat-fields of Minnesota, instead of producing twenty-five bushels to the acre upon an average throughout the State, will not yield ten, which is the product in Ohio; and yet, with a systematic rotation of crops and application of fertilizers, the present marvellous richness of the soil can be maintained forever.

"Do the tame grasses flourish?"

Splendidly; I never saw finer fields of timothy than along the line of the St. Paul and Pacific Railroad, west of Minneapolis. White clover seems to spring up of its own accord. I remember that I saw it growing luxuriantly along a pathway in the Red River Valley, and by the side of the military road leading through the woods to Lake Superior. Hay is very abundant, and exceedingly cheap in Minnesota. I doubt if there is a State in the Union that has a greater breadth of first-class grass-lands. Hon. Thomas Clarke, Assistant State Geologist, estimates the area of meadow-lands between the St. Croix and the Mississippi, and south of Sandy Lake, at a million acres. He says: "Some of these are very extensive, and bear a luxuriant growth of grass, often five or six feet in height. It is coarse, but sweet, and is said to make excellent hay."

I passed through some of those meadows, and can speak from personal observation. I saw many acres that would yield two tons to the acre. The grasses are native, flat-leaved, foul-meadow and blue-joint, just such as I used to swing a scythe through years ago in a meadow in New Hampshire which furnished a fair quality of hay. The time will come when those lands will be valuable, although they are not held very high at present. A few years ago the Kankakee swamps in Illinois and Indiana were valueless, but now they yield many thousand tons of hay, and are rising in the market.

"How about fruit? I don't want to go where I cannot raise fruit."

Those native to the soil are strawberries, raspberries, blackberries, gooseberries, huckleberries, cherries, and plums. I picked all of these upon the prairies and along the streams while there. The wild plum is very abundant, and in the fall of the year you will see thousands of bushels in the markets at St. Paul and Minneapolis. They make an excellent sauce or preserve.

Minnesota may be called the Cranberry State. Many farmers make more money from their cranberry-meadows than from their wheat-fields. The marshes in the northern section of the State are covered with vines, and the lands along the St. Croix yield abundantly.

Mr. Clarke, the geologist, says: "There are 256,000 acres of cranberry-marsh in the triangle between the St. Croix and Mississippi, and bounded north by the St. Louis and Prairie Rivers! The high price paid for this delicious fruit makes its cultivation very profitable in Minnesota, as well as in New Jersey and on Cape Cod."

"Can apples be raised? I am fond of them, and should consider it a drawback if I could not have an apple-orchard," said the persistent Mr. Blotter.

I understand that till within a year or two the prospect for apples was not very encouraging. The first orchards were from Illinois nurseries, and it was not till native stocks were started that success attended the fruit-growers' efforts; but now they have orchards as thrifty and bountiful as any in the country. At the last State Fair held at Rochester, one fruit-grower had fifty bushels on exhibition, and two hundred more at home. It was estimated that the yield in Winona County last year was thirty thousand bushels.*

The St. Paul Press, noticing the display of fruits at the Ramsay and Hennipen County Fair, says: "These two fairs have set at rest the long-mooted

* These and many other facts relating to Minnesota are obtained from "Minnesota as it is in 1870," by J. W. McClung, of St. Paul, — an exceedingly valuable work, crammed with information.

question, whether Minnesota is an apple-growing State. Over two hundred varieties of the apple, exclusive of the crab species, were exhibited at Minneapolis, and a large number at St. Paul, of the finest development and flavor, and this fact will give an immense impetus to fruit-growing in our State."

The following varieties were exhibited at the last meeting of the Fruit-Growers' Association, of Winona County: The Duchess of Oldenburg, Utter's Large, Early Red, Sweet June, Perry Russet, Fall Stripe, Keswick Codlin, Red Astracan, Plum Cider, Phœnix, Wagner, Ben Davis, German Bough, Carolina Red June, Bailey Sweet, St. Lawrence, Sops of Wine, Seek-no-further, Famuse, Price Sweet, Pomme Grise, Tompkins County King, Northern Spy, Golden Russet, Sweet Pear, Yellow Ingestrie, Yellow Bellflower, Lady Finger, Raule's Jannet, Kirkbridge White, Janiton, Dumelow, Winter Wine Sap, Chronicle, Fall Wine Sap, Rosseau, Colvert, Benoni, Red Romanite.

Many of the above are raised in New England, so that those people who may cut loose from the East need not be apprehensive that they are bidding good by forever to the favorite fruits that have been a comfort as well as a luxury in their former homes.

"I take it that grapes do not grow there; it must be too far north," said my visitor.

On the contrary, they are indigenous. You find wild grapes along the streams, and in the gardens around St. Paul and Minneapolis you will see many of the cultivated varieties bearing magnificent clusters on the luxuriant vines.

"How about corn, rye, oats, and other grains; can they be raised with profit?"

The following figures, taken from the official report made to the last legislature of the products for 1869, will show the capabilities of the soil:—

			Average per Acre.
Wheat,	18,500,000	bushels,	18½
Corn,	6,125,000	"	35
Oats,	11,816,400	"	43
Potatoes,	2,745,000	"	90
Barley,	625,000	"	30.6
Rye,	58,000	"	18
Buckwheat,	28,000	"	16
Hay,	430,000	tons,	2.08
Wool,	390,000	pounds.	
Butter,	5,600,000	"	
Cheese,	145,000	"	
Sorghum,	80,000	gallons syrup.	
Maple Sugar,	300,000	pounds.	
Flax,	170,000	"	

From this it would seem that the State is destined to be one of the most productive in the Union.

"Have they good schools out there?"

Just as good as in New England. Two sections of land are set aside for the common-school fund.

The entire amount of school lands in the State will be three million acres.

These are sold at the rate of five dollars per acre, and the money invested in State or government bonds. Governor Marshall, in his last message, estimated the sum ultimately to be derived from the lands at sixteen million dollars. A school tax of two mills on the dollar is levied, which, with the interest from the fund, gives a liberal amount for education.

"At what season of the year ought a man to go West?"

That depends very much upon what you intend to do. If you are going to farming, and intend to settle upon the prairies, you must be there in season to break up your ground in July. If the sod is turned when the grass is full of juices, it decays quickly, and your ground will be in good condition for next year's ploughing. If you go into the timbered lands along the Lake Superior and Mississippi Railroad, or along that of the Northern Pacific, you can go any time; but men having families will do well to go in advance and select their future home, and make some preparations before cutting loose from the old one.

"Which is the best way to go?"

You will find either of the great trunk railroads leading westward comfortable routes, and their rates of fare do not greatly vary.

"Do you think that the State will have a rapid development?"

If the past is any criterion for the future, its growth will be unparalleled. Twenty years only have passed since it was organized as a Territory. The population in 1850 was 5,330; in 1860 it was 172,022; in 1865, by the State census, 250,099. The census of 1870 will give more than half a million. The tide of emigration is stronger at the present time than it ever has been before, and the construction of the various railroads, the liberal policy of the State, its munificent school-fund, the richness of the lands, the abundance of pure, fresh water, the delightful climate, the situation of the State in connection with the trans-continental line of railway, altogether will give Minnesota rapid advancement. Of the North-west as of a pumpkin-vine during the hot days and warm nights of midsummer, we may say that we can almost see it grow! Look at the increase of wealth as represented by real and personal estates:—

1850	$ 806,437
1855	10,424,157
1860	36,753,408
1865	45,127,318
1868	75,795,366

From the report of the Assistant Secretary of State made to the Legislature in January, 1870, we have the following facts:—

Total tilled acres, ...	1,690,000
Value of real estate, ...	$ 120,000,000
" " personal property, . . .	65,000,000
" " live stock, ...	15,561,887
" " agricultural productions, . .	25,000,000
" " annual manufactures, . .	11,000,000
Amount of school-fund, ...	2,371,199

Not only is Minnesota to have a rapid development, but Dakota as well. Civilization is advancing up the Missouri. Emigrants are moving on through Yankton and taking possession of the rich lands of that section, and the present year will see the more northern tide pouring into the Red River Valley, which Professor Hind called the Paradise of the Northwest.

"How much will it cost me to reach Minnesota, and get started on a farm?"

The fare from Boston to St. Paul will be from $ 35 to $ 40. If you go into the timbered regions, you will have lumber enough near at hand to build your house, and it will take a great many sturdy strokes to get rid of the oaks and pines. If you go upon the prairies, you will have to obtain lumber from a distance. The prices at Minneapolis are all the way from $ 12 to $ 45 per thousand, according to quality. Shingles cost from $ 3.50 to $ 4.50.

Most of the farmers begin with a very small house, containing two or three rooms. They do not start with much furniture. We who are accustomed to hot and cold water, bath-room, and all the modern conveniences of houses in the city, might think it rather hard at first to use a tin wash-basin on a bench out-doors, and ladies might find it rather awkward to go up to their chamber on a ladder; but we can accommodate ourselves to almost anything, especially when we are working towards independence. Settlers start with small houses, for a good deal of lumber is required for fencing. A fence around forty acres requires 1,700 rails, 550 posts, and a keg of large nails. The farmers do not dig holes, but sharpen the lower ends of the posts and drive them down with a beetle. Two men by this process will fence in forty acres in a very short time. Such fences are for temporary use, but will stand for several years, — till the settler has made headway enough to replace them with others more substantial. You will want horses and oxen. A span of good farm horses will cost $ 250; a yoke of good oxen, $ 125. Cows are worth from $ 20 to $ 50.

Carpenters, masons, and mechanics command high prices, — from $ 2 to $ 4.50 per day. Farm laborers can be hired for $ 20 to $ 25 per month.

"What section of the Northwest is advancing most rapidly?"

The southern half of Minnesota. As yet there are no settlements in the northern counties. Draw a line from Duluth to Fort Abercrombie, and you will have almost the entire population south of that line. A few families are living in Otter-Tail County, north of that line, and there are a few more in the Red River Valley.

Two years hence there will probably be many thousand inhabitants in the northern counties; the fertility of the Red River lands and the construction of two railroads cannot fail of attracting settlers in that direction. There is far more first quality of agricultural land now held by government in the northwestern counties than in any other section of the State. The land-office for that region is at Alexandria in Douglas County. The vacant land subject to pre-emption as per share in the eleven counties composing the district amounts to 10,359,000 acres, nearly the same area as Massachusetts and New Hampshire together. Take a glance at the counties.

Douglas. — Four years ago it did not contain a single inhabitant, but now it has a population of about 5,000! The county has an area of twenty townships, 460,000 acres, and about 250,000 are still held by government.

Grant. — It lies west of Douglas. We passed through it on our way to the Red River. The main line of the St. Paul and Pacific Railroad will run through the southwestern township this year. There are 295,000 acres still vacant.

Otter-Tail. — We travelled through this county

9*

on our return from Dakota, and were serenaded by the Germans in our camp on the bank of Rush Lake. It contains 1,288,000 acres, of which 850,000 are held by government. This county is abundantly supplied with timber, — pine as well as oak, and other of the hard woods. There are numerous lakes and ponds, and several fine mill-sites. The soil is excellent. The lakes abound with whitefish. In 1868 the population was 800. Now it may be set down at 2,000.

Wilkin. — This county is on the Red River. It was once called Andy Johnson, but now bears the name of Wilkin. There you may take your choice of 650,000 acres of fertile lands. You can find timber on the streams, or you may float it down from Otter-Tail. The St. Paul and Pacific Railroad will be constructed through the county during the year 1870.

Clay. — North of Wilkin on the Red River is Clay County, containing 650,000 acres of government land, all open to settlement. The Northern Pacific Railroad will probably strike the Red River somewhere in this county. The distance from Duluth will be two hundred and twenty-five miles, and the settler there will be as near market as the people of central Illinois or eastern Iowa.

Polk.—The next county north contains 2,480,000 acres, unsurpassed for fertility, well watered by the Red, the Wild Rice, Marsh, Sand Hill, and Red

Lake Rivers. The county is half as large as Massachusetts, and is as capable of sustaining a dense population as the kingdom of Belgium or the valley of the Ganges. The southern half will be accommodated by the Northern Pacific Railroad. Salt springs abound on the Wild Rice River, and the State has reserved 23,000 acres of the saline territory.

Pembina.—The northwestern county of the State contains 2,263,000 acres, all held by government.

Becker. — This county lies north of Otter-Tail. We passed through it on our way from the Red River to the head-waters of the Buffalo. (Description, p. 113.) It is a region surpassingly beautiful. The Northern Pacific Railroad will pass through it, and there you may find 435,000 acres of rolling prairie and timbered hills. Probably there are not fifty settlers in the county. A large portion of these northwestern counties are unsurveyed, but that will not debar you from pre-empting a homestead.

"How about the southwestern section of the State?" asked my visitor.

I cannot speak from personal observation beyond Blue Earth County, where the Minnesota River crooks its elbow and turns northeast; but from what I have learned I have reason to believe that the lands there are just as fertile as those already settled nearer the Mississippi, and they will be made available by the railroad now under construction from St. Paul to Sioux City.

"Can a man with five hundred dollars make a beginning out there with a reasonable prospect of success?"

Yes, provided he has good pluck, and is willing to work hard and to wait. If he can command one thousand dollars, he can do a great deal better than he can with half that sum.

If you were to go out sixty miles beyond St. Paul to Darsel, on the St. Paul and Pacific Railroad you would see a farm worked by seven sisters. The oldest girl is about twenty-five, the youngest fifteen. They lived in Ohio, but their father and mother were invalids, and for their benefit came to Minnesota in April, 1867, and secured a hundred and sixty acres of land under the Homestead Law. The neighbors turned out and helped them build a log-house, and the girls went to work on the farm. Last year (1869) they had forty acres under cultivation, and sold 900 bushels of potatoes, 500 bushels of corn, 200 of wheat, 250 of turnips, 200 of beets, besides 1,100 cabbage-heads, and about two hundred dollars' worth of other garden products. They hired men to split rails for fencing, and also to plough the land; but all the other work has been done by the girls, who are hale and hearty, and find time to read the weekly papers and magazines. The mother of these girls made the following remark to a gentleman who visited the farm: "The girls are not fond of the hard work they have had to do to get the farm started, but they are not ashamed of it. We were too poor to keep together, and live in a town. We could not make a living there, but here we have become comfortable and independent. We tried to give the girls a good education, and they all read and write, and find a little spare time to read books and papers."

These plucky girls have set a good example to young men who want to get on in the world.

Perhaps I am too enthusiastic over the future prospects of the region between Lake Superior and the Pacific, but having travelled through Kansas, Nebraska, Utah, and Nevada, I have had an opportunity to contrast the capabilities of the two sections. Kansas has magnificent prairies, and so has Nebraska, but there are no sparkling ponds, no wood-fringed lakes, no gurgling brooks abounding with trout. The great want of those States is water. The soil is exceedingly fertile, even in Utah and Nevada, though white with powdered alkali, but they are valueless for want of moisture. In marked contrast to all this is the great domain of the Northwest. For a few years the tide of emigration will flow, as it is flowing now, into the central States; but when the lands there along the rivers and streams are all taken up, the great river of human life, setting towards the Pacific, will be turned up the Missouri, the Assinniboine, and the Saskatchawan. The climate, the resources of the country, the capabilities for a varied industry, and the configuration of the continent, alike indicate it.

I am not sure that Mr. Blotter accepted all this, but he has gone to Minnesota with his wife, turning his back on a dry-goods counting-house to obtain a home on the prairies.

CHAPTER XI.

NORTHERN PACIFIC RAILROAD.

THE statesman, the political economist, or any man who wishes to cast the horoscope of the future of this country, must take into consideration the great lakes, and their connection with the Mississippi, the Missouri, and the Columbia Rivers, and those portions of the continent drained by these water-ways.

Communities do not grow by chance, but by the operation of physical laws. Position, climate, mountains, valleys, rivers, lakes, arable lands, coal, wood, iron, silver, and gold are predestinating forces in a nation's history, decreeing occupation, character, power, and influence.

Lakes and navigable streams are natural highways for trade and traffic; valleys are natural avenues; mountains are toll-gates set up by nature. He who passes over them must pay down in sweat and labor.

Humboldt discussed the question a third of a century ago. "The natural highways of nations," said he, "will usually be along the great water-courses."

It impressed me deeply, as long ago as 1846,

when the present enormous railway system of the continent had hardly begun to be developed. Spreading out a map of the Western Hemisphere, I then saw that from Cape Horn to Behring's Strait there was only one river-system that could be made available to commerce on the Pacific coast. In South America there is not a stream as large as the Merrimac flowing into the Pacific. The waves of the ocean break everywhere against the rocky wall of the Andes.

In North America the Colorado rises on the pinnacle of the continent, but it flows through a country upheaved by volcanic fires during the primeval years. Its chasms and cañons are the most stupendous on the globe. The course of the stream is southwest to the Gulf of California, out of the line of direction for commerce.

The only other great stream of the Pacific coast is the Columbia, whose head-waters are in a line with those of the Missouri, the Mississippi, the Red River of the North, and Lake Superior.

This one feature of the physical geography of the continent was sufficient to show me that the most feasible route for a great continental highway between the Atlantic and the Pacific must be from Lake Superior to the valley of the Columbia.

In childhood I had read the travels of Lewis and Clark over and over again, till I could almost repeat the entire volume, and, remembering their glowing accounts of the country,—the fertility of the valley of the Yellowstone, the easy passage from the Jefferson fork of the Missouri to the Columbia, and the mildness of the winters on the Western slope, the conviction was deepened that the best route for a railway from the lakes to the Pacific would be through one of the passes of the Rocky Mountains at the head-waters of the Missouri.

Doubtless, many others observant of the physical geography of the continent had arrived at the same natural conclusion. Seven years later the government surveys were made along several of the parallels, that from Lake Superior to the Columbia being under the direction of Governor I. I. Stevens. Jeff Davis was then Secretary of War, and his report set forth the northern route as being virtually impracticable. It was, according to his representation, incapable of sustaining population. A careful study of Governor Stevens's Report, and a comparison with the reports along the more southern lines, showed that the Secretary of War had deliberately falsified the statements of Governor Stevens and his assistants. While the surveys were being made, Mr. Edwin F. Johnson, of Middletown, Conn., the present chief engineer of the Pacific Railroad, published a pamphlet which set forth in a clear and forcible manner the natural advantages of the route by the Missouri.

In 1856 the British government sent out an exploring expedition under Captain Palliser, whose report upon the attractions of British America, the richness of the soil, the ease with which a road could be constructed to the Pacific through British territory, created great interest in Parliament.

"The accomplishment of such a scheme," said Mr. Roebuck, "would unite England with Vancouver Island and with China, and they would be enabled widely to extend the civilization of England, and he would boldly assert that the civilization of England was greater than that of America."

"Already," said the Colonial Secretary, Lord Lytton, better known to American readers as Bulwer, "in the large territory which extends west of the Rocky Mountains, from the American frontier and up to the skirts of the Russian dominions, we are laying the foundations of what may become hereafter a magnificent abode of the human race."

There was a tone about these speeches that stirred my blood, and I prepared a pamphlet for circulation entitled "The Great Commercial Prize," which was published in 1858. It was a plea for the immediate construction of a railway up the valley of the Missouri, and down the Columbia to Puget Sound, over the natural highway, giving facts and figures in regard to its feasibility; but I was laughed at for my pains, and set down as a visionary by the press.

It is gratifying to have our good dreams come to pass. That which was a dream of mine in 1846 is in process of fulfilment in 1870. The discovery of gold in California and the building up of a great city demanded the construction of a railroad to San Francisco, which was chartered in 1862, and which has been constructed with unparalleled rapidity, and is of incalculable service to the nation.

The charter of the Northern Pacific was granted in 1864, and approved by President Lincoln on the 2d of July of that year. Government granted no subsidy of bonds, but gave ten alternate sections per mile on each side of the road in the States and twenty on each side of the line in the Territories through which it might pass.

Though the franchise was accompanied by this liberal land-grant, it has been found impossible to undertake a work of such magnitude till the present time. Nearly every individual named as corporators in the charter, with the exception of Governor J. G. Smith, its present President, Judge R. D. Rice, the Vice-President, and a few others, abandoned it under the many difficulties and discouragements that beset the enterprise. The few gentlemen who held on studied the geography of the country, and their faith in the future of the

Northwest was strengthened. A year ago they were fortunate enough to find other men as enthusiastic as themselves over the resources and capabilities of the region between Lake Superior and the Pacific, —Messrs. Jay Cooke & Co., the well-known bankers of Philadelphia, whose names are indissolubly connected with the history of the country as its successful financial agents at a time when the needs of the nation were greatest; Messrs. Edgar Thompson and Thomas A. Scott, of the Pennsylvania Central Railroad; Mr. G. W. Cass, of the Pittsburg and Fort Wayne; Mr. B. P. Cheney, of Wells, Fargo, & Co.; Mr. William B. Ogden, of the Chicago and Northwestern Road; Mr. Stinson, of Chicago; and other gentlemen, most of whom are practical railroad men of large experience and far-reaching views.

Mr. Cooke became the financial agent of the company, and from that hour the advancement of the enterprise may be dated. It required but a few days to raise a subscription of $ 5,600,000 among the capitalists of the country to insure the building of the road from Lake Superior to the Red River, to which place it is now under construction. The year 1871 will probably see it constructed to the Missouri River, thus opening easy communication with Montana. The gentlemen who have taken hold of the work contemplate its completion to the Pacific in three years.

The line laid down upon the accompanying map only indicates the general direction of the road. It is the intention of the company to find the best route across the continent,—direct in course, with easy grades,—and this can only be ascertained by a thorough exploration of the valley of the Yellowstone, the passes at the head-waters of the Missouri, the valley of the Columbia, and the shores and harbors of Puget Sound.

The engineers are setting their stakes from Lake Superior to the Red River, and laborers with spade and shovel are following them. Imagination bounds onward over the prairies, across the mountains, down the valley of the Columbia, and beholds the last rail laid, the last spike driven, and a new highway completed across the continent.

I think of myself as being upon the locomotive, for a run from the lakes to the western ocean.

Our starting-point on the lake is 600 feet above the sea. We gain the height of land between the lake and the Mississippi by a gentle asçent. Thirty-one miles out from Duluth we find the waters trickling westward to the Mississippi. There we are 558 feet above Lake Superior. It is almost a dead level, as the engineers say, from that point to the Mississippi, which is 552 feet above the lake at Crow Wing, or 1,152 feet above tide-water. The distance between the lake and Crow Wing is about a hundred miles, and the country is so level that it would be an easy matter to dig a canal and turn the Mississippi above Crow Wing eastward into the waters that reach the sea through the St. Lawrence.

The Leaf Hills are 267 feet higher than the Mississippi, and the ascent is only seven feet to the mile, — so slight that the engineers on the locomotive reckon it as level grade. These hills form the divide between the Mississippi and the Red River. Straight on, over the level valley of the Red River, westward to the summit of the rolling prairies between the Red River and the Missouri, the locomotive speeds its way. Gradually we rise till we are 2,400 feet above tide-water, — the same elevation that is reached on the Union Pacific 250 miles west of Omaha.

A descent of 400 feet carries us to the Missouri. We wind up its fertile valley to the richer bottom-lands of the Yellowstone, over a route so level that at the mouth of the Big Horn we are only 2,500 feet above tide-water. The Yellowstone flows with a swifter current above the Big Horn. We are approaching the mountains, and must pass the ridge of land that separates the Yellowstone from the upper waters of the Missouri. It lies 950 miles west of Lake Superior, and the summit is 4,500 feet above the sea. Through the entire distance, thus far, there have been no grades greater than those of the Illinois Central and other prairie railroads of the West. Crossing the Missouri we are at the back-bone of the continent, depressed here like the vertebra of a hollow-backed horse. We may glide through the Deer Lodge Pass by a grade of fifty feet, at an altitude of only 5,000 feet above tide-water.

Mr. Milnor Roberts, civil engineer, approached it from the west, and this is his description of the Pass: —

"Considered as a railroad route, this valley is remarkably favorable, the rise from Deer Lodge City to the pass or divide between the waters of the Pacific and Atlantic being quite gentle, and even on the last few miles, the summit, about 5,000 feet above the sea, may be attained without employing a gradient exceeding fifty feet to the mile, with a moderate cut. The whole forty miles from Deer Lodge City to the summit of the Rocky Mountains by this route can be built as cheaply as roads are built through prairie countries generally. A little more work will be required in passing to the east side from this side, down Divide Creek to Wisdom or Big Hole River; but the line will be highly favorable on an average all the way to the Jefferson Fork of the Missouri River. This favorable pass comes into connection more particularly with the Yellowstone Valley route to the main Missouri Valley. A remarkable circumstance connected with this pass will convey a very clear view of its peculiarly favorable character. Private parties engaged in gold mining, in the gold-fields which exist abundantly on both sides of the Rocky Mountains, have dug a ditch across this summit which is only eighteen feet deep at the apex of the divide, through which they carry the waters of 'Divide Creek,' a tributary of the Missouri, across to the Pacific side, where it is used in gold-washing, and the waste water passes into the Pacific Ocean. This has been justly termed highway robbery."

There are half a dozen passes nearly as low, — Mullan's, Blackfoot, Lewis and Clark's, Cadotte's, and the Marias.

Going through the Deer Lodge Pass, we find that the stream changes its name very often before reaching the Pacific. The little brook on the summit of the divide, turbid with the washings of the gold-mines, is called the Deer Lodge Creek. Twenty-five miles farther on it is joined by a small stream that trickles from the summit of Mullan's Pass, near Helena, and the two form the Hell Gate, just as the Pemigewasset and Winnipesaukee form the Merrimac in New Hampshire, receiving its name from the many Indian fights that have taken place in its valley, where the Blackfeet and Nez Percés have had many a battle. The stream bears the name of Hell Gate for about eighty miles before being joined by the Blackfoot, which flows from the mountains in the vicinity of Cadotte's and Lewis and Clark's Passes.

A little below the junction it empties into the Bitter Root, which, after a winding course of a hundred miles, is joined by the Flathead, that comes down from Flathead Lake and the country around Marias Pass. The united streams below the junction take the name of Clark's River, which has a circuitous course northward, running for a little distance into British America, then back again through a wide plain till joined by the Snake, and the two become the Columbia, pouring a mighty flood westward to the ocean. The line of the road does not follow the river to the boundary between the United States and the British Possessions, but strikes across the plain of the Columbia.

The characteristics of Clark's River and the surrounding country are thus described by Mr. Roberts: —

"Clark's River has a flow in low water at least six times greater than the low-water flow of the Ohio River between Pittsburg and Wheeling; and while its fall is slight, considered with reference to railroad grades, it is so considerable as to afford a great number of water-powers, whose future value must be very great, — an average of eleven feet per mile.

"Around Lake Pend d'Oreille, and for some miles

westward, and all along Clark's River above the lake as far as we traversed it, there is a magnificent region of pine, cypress, hemlock, tamarack, and cedar timber, many of the trees of prodigious size. I measured one which was thirty-four feet in circumference, and a number that were over twenty-seven feet, and saw hundreds, as we passed along, that were from twenty to twenty-five feet in circumference, and from two hundred to two hundred and fifty feet high. A number of valleys containing large bodies of this character of timber enter Clark's River from both sides, and the soil of these valleys is very rich. Clark's River Valley itself is for much of the distance confined by very high hills approaching near to the stream in many places; but there are sufficient sites for cities and farms adjacent to water-powers of the first class, and not many years can elapse after the opening of a railroad through this valley till it will exhibit a combination of industries and population analogous to those which now mark the Lehigh, the Schuylkill, the Susquehanna, and the Pomroy region of the Ohio River. Passing along its quiet scenes of to-day, we can see in the near future the vast change which the enterprise of man will bring. That which was once the work of half a century is now the product of three or four years. Indeed, in a single year after the route of this Northern

Pacific Railroad shall have been determined, and the work fairly begun, all this region, now so calm and undisturbed, will be teeming with life instilled into it by hardy pioneers from the Atlantic and from the Pacific.

"Passing along the Flathead River for a short distance, we entered the valley of the Jocko River. The same general remarks concerning Clark's River Valley are applicable to the Flathead and Bitter Root Valleys. The climate, the valleys, the timber, the soil, the water-powers, all are here, awaiting only the presence of the industrious white man to render to mankind the benefits implanted in them by a beneficent Creator."

The entire distance from Lake Superior by the Yellowstone Valley to the tide-waters of the Pacific below the cascades of the Columbia will be about eighteen hundred miles. It is nearly the same distance to Seattle, on Puget Sound, by the Snoqualmie Pass of the Cascade Range.

The Union Pacific line has had no serious obstruction from snow since its completion. It has suffered no more than other roads of the country, and its trains have arrived as regularly at Omaha and Sacramento as the trains of the New York Central at Buffalo or Albany. That the Northern Pacific road will be quite as free from snow-blockades will be manifest by a perusal of the following paragraphs from the report of Mr. Roberts:—

"There is evidence enough to show that the line of road on the general route herein described will, in ordinary winters, be much less encumbered with snow where it crosses the mountains than are the passes at more southerly points, which are much more elevated above the sea. The difference of five or six degrees of latitude is more than compensated by the reduced elevation above the sea-level, and the climatic effect of the warm ocean-currents from the equator, already referred to, ameliorating the seasons from the Pacific to the Rocky Mountains. An examination of the profile of the Union Pacific and Central Pacific lines between Omaha, on the Missouri River, and Sacramento, California, a distance of 1,775 miles, shows that there are four main summits, — Sherman Summit, on the Black Hills, about 550 miles from Omaha, 8,235 feet above the sea; one on the Rocky Mountains, at Aspen Summit, about 935 miles from Omaha, 7,463 feet; one at Humboldt Mountain, about 1,245 miles from Omaha, 6,076 feet; and another on the Sierra Nevada, only 105 miles from the western terminus at Sacramento, 7,062 feet; whilst from a point west of Cheyenne, 520 miles from Omaha, to Wasatch, 970 miles from Omaha, a continuous length of 450 miles, every portion of the graded road is more than 6,000 feet above the sea, being about 1,000 feet on this long distance higher than the highest summit grade on the Northern Pacific Railroad route; whilst for the corresponding distance on the Northern Pacific line the average elevation is under 3,000 feet, or *three thousand feet* lower than the Sherman Summit on the Pacific line.

"On the Union Pacific road the profile also shows that for 900 continuous miles, from Sidney westward, the road has an average height of over 5,000 feet, and the lowest spot on that distance is more than 4,000 feet above the sea, whereas on the Northern route only about sixty miles at most are as high as 4,000 feet, and the corresponding distance of 900 miles, extending from the mouth of the Yellowstone to the valley of Clark's River, is, on an average, about 3,000 feet lower than the Union Pacific line. Allowing that 1,000 feet of elevation causes a decrease of temperature of three degrees, this would be a difference of nine degrees. There is, therefore, a substantial reason for the circumstance, now well authenticated, that the snows on the Northern route are much less troublesome than they are on the Union Pacific and Central Pacific routes" (Report, p. 43).

That the Northern Pacific can be economically worked is demonstrated by a comparison of its grades with those of the line already constructed. The comparison is thus presented by Mr. Roberts:—

"The grades on the route across through the State of Minnesota and Territory of Dakota to the Missouri River will not be materially dissimilar to those on the other finished railroads south of it, passing from Chicago to Sioux City, Council Bluffs, etc.; namely, undulating within the general limit of about forty feet per mile, although it may be deemed advisable, at a few points for short distances, to run to a maximum of one foot per hundred or fifty-three feet per mile. There is sufficient knowledge of this portion of the route to warrant this assumption. And beyond the Missouri, along the valley of the Yellowstone, to near the Bozeman Pass, there is no known reason for assuming any higher limits. In passing Bozeman Summit of the Belt Range, and in going up the eastern side of the Rocky Mountains, it may be found advisable to adopt a somewhat higher gradient for a few miles in overcoming those summits. This, however, can only be finally determined after careful surveys.

The highest ground encountered between Lake Superior and the Missouri River, at the mouth of the Yellowstone, is only 2,300 feet above the sea; the low summit of the Rocky Mountains is but little over 5,000 feet, and the Bozeman Pass, through the Belt Range, is assumed to be about 500 feet lower. The height of the country upon which the line is traced, and upon which my estimate of cost is based, may be approximately stated thus, beginning at Lake Superior, going westward:—

	Miles.	Average height above the sea.
To Dakota Valley, . .	300 . .	1,200 feet.
Yellowstone River, .	300 . .	2,200 "
Along Yellowstone, . .	400 . .	2,500 "
Flathead Valley, . .	300 . .	3,500 "
Lewis or Snake River, .	200 . .	3,000 "
Puget Sound, . .	500 . .	400 "
	2,000	

Compare this with the profiles of the finished line of the Union and Central Pacific roads. Properly, the comparison should be made from Chicago, the eastern water terminus of Lake Michigan, of the Omaha line. There are, on that route, approximately, as follows:—

	Miles.	Average height above the sea.
From Chicago to Omaha, .	500 . .	1,000 feet
Near Cheyenne, . .	500 .	3,300 "
Cooper's, ...	100 . .	7,300 "
Promontory Point, . .	485 .	6,200 "
Humboldt, ...	406 . .	4,750 "
Reno, ...	130 .	4,000 "
Auburn, ...	118 . .	4,400 "
Sacramento, ...	36 .	300 "
San Francisco, . . .	100 . .	50 "
Chicago to San Francisco	2,375	

"On the Northern Pacific line there need be but two principal summits, whilst on the other there are four, the lowest of which is about a thousand feet higher than the highest on the northern route. If, therefore, the roads were the same length between the Pacific waters and the great lakes and navigable rivers east of the Rocky Mountains, the advantage would be largely in favor of the Northern route; but this actual distance is three hundred and seventy-five miles less, and the equated distance for ascents and descents in its favor will be very considerable" (Report, p. 45).

From the explorations and surveys already made by the engineers, it is believed that there need be no gradient exceeding sixty feet per mile between Lake Superior and the Pacific Ocean. If such be the fact, it will enable the company to transport freight much more cheaply than the central line can carry it, where the grades are one hundred and sixteen feet to the mile, over the Sierra Nevada Range. To those who never have had time to examine the subject, the following tabular statement in regard to the power of a thirty-ton engine on different grades will be interesting. An engine weighing thirty tons will draw loaded cars on different grades as follows: —

On a level	94 cars
10 feet per mile ascending . .	56 "
20 " " " " . .	40 "
30 " " " " . . .	30½ "
40 " " " " . .	25 "
50 " " " " . . .	20½ "
60 " " " " . .	17 "

70	feet per mile ascending . . .	15 cars.
80	" " " " . . .	13 "
90	" " " " . . .	11½ "
100	" " " " . . .	10 "
110	" " " " . . .	8½ "
120	" " " " . . .	6 "

A full car-load is reckoned at seven tons. It has been found in the operation of railroads that an engine which will move one hundred and seventeen tons on a grade sixty feet per mile will move only about fifty tons on a grade of one hundred and sixteen feet. A second glance at the diagram (p. 48) shows us that the sum of ascents and descents on the line already constructed must be vastly greater than that now under construction; and inasmuch as it is impossible to carry a load up or down hill without costing something, it follows that this road can be operated more economically than a line crossing four mountain-ranges, and the ultimate result will be a cheapening of transportation across the continent, and a great development of the Asiatic trade.

Throughout the entire distance between Lake Superior and the Pacific Ocean along the line, the husbandman may turn the sod with his plough, the herdsman fatten his flocks, the lumberman reap the harvest of the forests, or the miner gather golden ore.

A Bureau of Emigration is to be established by

the company, which will be of invaluable service to the emigrant.

Many persons in the Eastern and Middle States are desirous of moving to the Northwest, but it is hard to cut loose from old associations, to leave home and friends and strike out alone upon the prairie; they want company. The human race is gregarious. There are not many who care to be hermits, and most of us prefer society to solitude.

This feature of human nature is to be kept in view, and it will be the aim of the Bureau of Emigration to offer every facility to those seeking new homes to take their friends with them.

Upon the completion of every twenty-five miles of road, the company will be put in possession of forty sections of land per mile. The government will hold the even-numbered sections, and the company those bearing the odd numbers.

The land will be surveyed, plotted, and the distinctive features of each section described. Emigration offices are to be established in our own country as well as abroad, where maps, plans, and specifications will be found.

One great drawback to the settlement of the prairie lands of Illinois and Iowa has been the want of timber for the construction of houses. Persons with limited means, having only their own hands, found it hard to get started on a treeless prairie. Their first work is to obtain a house. The

Bureau propose to help the man who is anxious to help himself on in the world, by putting up a portable house for him on the land that he may select. The houses will be small, but they will serve till the settler can get his farm fenced in, his ground ploughed, and two or three crops of wheat to market. The abundance of timber in Minnesota will enable the company to carry out this new feature of emigration.

It will be an easy matter for a family from Lowell, another from Methuen, a third from Andover, a fourth from Reading, a fifth from Haverhill, to select their land in a body and start a Massachusetts colony in the Seat of Empire.

Far better this method than for each family to go out by itself. Going as a colony they will carry the moral atmosphere of their old homes with them. They will have a school in operation the week after their arrival. And on Sabbath morning, swelling upward on the summer air, sweeter than the lay of lark amid the flowers, will ascend the songs of the Sunday school established in their new home. Looking forward with ardent hope to prosperous years, they will still look beyond the earthly to the heavenly, and sing, —

"My heavenly home is bright and fair,
Nor pain nor death shall enter there."

This is no fancy sketch; it is but a description of what has been done over and over again in

Ohio, Indiana, Illinois, Iowa, and all the Western States. The Northern Pacific Railroad Company want their lands settled by an industrious, thrifty, energetic people, who prize everything that goes to make up the highest grade of civilization, and they are ready to render such help as no colonies have yet had.

The land will be sold to actual settlers at low rates, and on liberal terms of payment. The portable houses will be sold at cost, transported on the cars, and set up for the colonists if they desire it.

The Bureau will be put in operation as soon as it can be systematically organized, and I doubt not that thousands will avail themselves of its advantages to establish their future homes near a railroad which will give the shortest line across the continent, marked by low gradients, running through the lowest passes of the Rocky Mountains, through a country capable of cultivation all the way from the lakes to the Pacific.

Am I dreaming?

Across this belt of land between Lake Superior and the Pacific lies the world's great future highway. The physical features of this portion of the continent are favorable for the development of every element of a high civilization.

Take one more look at the map, and observe the situation of the St. Lawrence and the lakes, furnishing water-carriage for freight half-way from ocean to ocean, — the prairies extending to the base of the Rocky Mountains, — the one summit to be crossed, — the bays, inlets, and harbors of the Pacific shore laved by ocean currents and warmed by winds wafted from the equator to the Arctic Sea. Observe also the shortest lines of latitude.

The geographical position is in the main axial line of the world's grand commercial movement. San Francisco and Puget Sound are the two western gateways of the continent. Rapid as has been the advancement of civilization around the Golden Gate, magnificent as its future may be, yet equally grand and majestic will be the northern portal of the great Republic. Not only will it be on the shortest possible route between England and Asia, but it will be in the direct line between England and the Asiatic dominions of Russia.

While we are building our railroads westward from the Atlantic to the Pacific, the Emperor of Russia is extending his from the Ural Mountains eastward, down the valley of the Amoor, to open communication with China and Japan. The shortest route of travel round the world a few years hence will lie through the northern section of this continent and through Siberia. The Himalaya Range of mountains and the deserts of Central Asia will be impassible barriers to railroads between India and China, or Central Europe and the East; but the valley of the Amoor is fertile, and there is no fairer section of the Czar's dominions than Siberia. From Puget Sound straight across the Pacific will be found, a few years hence, the shortest route around the world.

Farm-houses dot the landscape, roses climb by cottage-doors, bees fill the air with their humming, bringing home to their hives the sweets gathered from far-off prairie-flowers; the prattle of children's voices floats upon the air, the verdant waste becomes an Eden, villages, towns, and cities spring into existence. A great metropolis rises upon the Pacific shore, where the winter air is laden with the perfume of ever-blooming flowers.

The ships of all nations lie at anchor in the land-locked bays, or shake out their sails for a voyage to the Orient. Steamships come and go, laden with the teas of China and Japan, the coffee of Java, the spices of Sumatra. I hear the humming of saws, the pounding of hammers, the flying of shuttles, the click and clatter of machinery. By every mill-stream springs up a town. The slopes are golden with ripening grain. The forest, the field, the mine, the river, alike yield their abundance to the ever-growing multitude.

Such is the outlook towards the future. Will the intellectual and moral development keep pace with the physical growth? If those are wanting, the advancement will be towards Sodom. The future man of the Northwest will have American, Norse, Celtic, and Saxon blood in his veins. His countenance, in the pure, dry, electric air, will be as fresh as the morning. His muscles will be iron, his nerves steel. Vigor will characterize his every action, — for climate gives quality to the blood, strength to the muscles, power to the brain. Indolence is characteristic of people living in the tropics, and energy of those in temperate zones.

The citizen of the Northwest will be a freeman. No shackles will bind him, nor will he wear a lock upon his lips. To the emigrant from the Old World the crossing of the ocean is an act of emancipation; it is like the Marseillaise, — it fires him with new hopes and aspirations.

"Here the free spirit of mankind at length
Throws its last fetters off, and who shall place
A limit to the giant's unchained strength,
Or curb his swiftness in the forward race?
For like the comet's way through infinite space,
Stretches the long untravelled path of light
Into the depth of ages; we may trace,
Distant, the brightening glory of its flight,
Till the receding rays are lost to human sight."

I do not look with desponding eyes into the future. The nations everywhere, — in Europe and Asia, — the new and the old, are moving onward and upward as never before, and America leads them. Railroads, steamships, school-houses, printing-presses, free platforms and pulpits, an open

Bible, are the propelling forces of the nineteenth century. It remains only for the Christian men and women of this country to give the Bible, the Sunday and the common school to the coming millions, to insure a greatness and grandeur to America far surpassing anything in human history.

It will not be for America alone; for, under the energizing powers of this age the entire human race is moving on towards a destiny unseen except to the eye of faith, but unmistakably grand and glorious.

I have been an observer of the civilization of Europe, and have seen the kindlings of new life, at the hands of England and the United States, in India and China; and through the drifting haze of the future I behold nations rising from the darkness of ancient barbarism into the light of modern civilization, and the radiant cross once reared on Calvary throwing its peaceful beams afar, — over ocean, valley, lake, river, and mountain, illuming all the earth.

Situated where the great stream of human life will pour its mightiest flood from ocean to ocean, beneficently endowed with nature's riches, and illumed by such a light, there will be no portion of all earth's wide domain surpassing in glory and grandeur this future Seat of Empire.

Cambridge: Printed by Welch, Bigelow, and Company.

THE FIRST DIVISION OF THE

St. Paul and Pacific Railroad Company.

LAND DEPARTMENT.

THE COMPANY NOW OFFERS FOR SALE

1,000,000 Acres of Land,

Located along their two Railroad Lines, viz.: From St. Paul, via St. Anthony, Anoka, St. Cloud, and Sauk Rapids, to Watab; and from St. Anthony, via Minneapolis, Wayzata, Crow River, Waverly, and Forest City, to the Western Boundary of the State.

THESE LANDS COMPRISE TIMBER, MEADOW, AND PRAIRIE LANDS,

And are all within easy distance of the Railroad, in the midst of considerable Settlements, convenient to Churches and Schools.

Inducement to Settlers.

The attention of persons whose limited means forbid the purchase of a homestead in the older States, is particularly invited to these lands. The farms are sold in tracts of 40 or 80 acres and upwards, at prices ranging from $5.00 to $10.00 per acre. Cash sales are always One Dollar per acre less than Credit sales. In the latter case 10 years are granted if required.

EXAMPLE. — 80 acres at $8.00 per acre, on long credit, — $640.00. A part payment on the principal is always desired, but in case the means of the settler are very limited, the Company allows him to pay only One Year's Interest down, dividing the principal in ten equal annual payments, with seven per cent interest each year on the unpaid balance:

	Int.	Prin.		Int.	Prin.
1st payment . . .	$44.80		7th payment . . .	$17.92	$64
2d "	40.32	$64	8th "	13.44	64
3d "	35.84	64	9th " . . .	8.96	64
4th "	31.36	64	10th "	4.48	64
5th " . . .	26.28	64	11th " . . .		64
6th "	22.40	64			

The purchaser has the privilege to pay up any time within the 10 years, thereby saving the payment of interest.

The same land may be purchased for $560.00 cash. Any other information will be furnished on application in person, or by letter, in English, French or German, addressed to

LAND COMMISSIONER,
First Division St. Paul & Pacific R. R. Co.,
SAINT PAUL, MINN.

"CARLETON'S" WORKS.

OUR NAGPORE COACH.

OUR NEW WAY ROUND THE WORLD;

OR,

WHERE TO GO AND WHAT TO SEE.

By CHARLES CARLETON COFFIN. Containing several full-page Maps, showing steamship lines and routes of travel, and profusely illustrated with more than 100 engravings, reproduced from photographs and original sketches. Crown octavo. Morocco Cloth, $3.00 ; Half Calf, $5.50 ; Library Edition, $3.50.

"In Mr. Charles C. Coffin we have a traveller after the latest and best transatlantic pattern. He has thrown himself thoroughly into the spirit of his age and race ; yet, while loyal to the backbone, and indorsing to the full his country's claims to present grandeur and future pre-eminence, he has a corner in his soul for the merits of other lands, and is open to the lessons of Old-World wisdom. Rapid as was his flight, and superficial as was his purview of the multitudinous objects that daily crowded his path, his powers of observation are, we are bound to say, keen and vigorous, and his judgments upon men and things both shrewd and impartial. Be it the aspects of nature, the historical monuments, the national traits, or the social idiosyncrasies that come before him, we find him invariably alive to what is most beautiful or august or original or piquant, as the case may be. He is at all times happy in hitting off the salient features, or picking out the weak spots, in local life and manners. . . . . The history of British rule in India, and the tokens of material and social advancement everywhere beside his path, are themes after the American's own heart. We have never seen a more graphic or telling sketch of Anglo-Indian life and characteristics within anything like the compass of Mr. Coffin's flying experiences . . . . Mr. Coffin's studies of life in China are eminently piquant and original. Nothing is too old or too new to escape his notice. . . . . The wood-cuts interspersed among his pages deserve a word of commendation. They are drawn with vigor and truth, often showing touches of quaint and quiet humor. Altogether, if there is nothing new under the sun, Our New Way Round the World shows there may be much novelty and freshness in the mode of telling even a thrice-told tale." — *Saturday Review* (*London*).

"The author of this interesting and valuable tour of the globe starts from New York, visits every city of note in Europe, sails from Marseilles to Alexandria, thence to Cairo, and Suez Canal, India, China, and Japan, returning by the way of California. Through this wide field for observation and research, his keen habits of characterization, and his vivid powers of description make him an exceedingly agreeable travelling companion. Mr. Coffin has the very happy faculty of giving to a really thrice-told tale of travel a freshness that carries the reader to the end of the volume with unabated interest. His tour in the interior of the British possessions in India is full of interest, — and his elaborate pictures of China at the present time are valuable, showing the actual character of the people; the tenacity of their prejudices, which appear to resist all innovation from 'outside barbarians,' is most graphically depicted, and is worthy the attention of our politicians and speculative philanthropists. The book on the whole is a valuable addition to our native literature, written as it is from a distinctive American stand-point view of foreign nations. Numerous spirited designs, illustrative of habits and manners, adorn the work, together with maps in abundance."— *N. Y. Express.*

"A model record of travel, over fields comparatively unknown. It combines, in a remarkable degree, skill and judgment in the selection of facts and points, with clearness, accuracy, and proportion in their statement: a natural ease and grace of expression, with a genial spirit, and a broad, true sympathy with everything human. A very large amount of instructive and attractive matter is compressed in its pages. The illustrations, too, are numerous, and all in admirable keeping with the narrative. In these, and in the clear, fair, readable type, the publishers have well done their part.

"We confess to a deeper, and consciously healthier interest in the perusal than in the reading of any similar volume. Very heartily, therefore, do we commend the book to the winter-evening family circle, sure that it will instruct and charm alike both young and old." — *N. Y. Christian World.*

"The book has many excellent illustrations, and is written with all the loveliness and instructiveness for which 'Carleton' became famous during the war, as a war correspondent of the *Boston Journal.* The book is gossipy and entertaining in a high degree, and will interest young and old." — *New York Evening Post.*

www.ingramcontent.com/pod-product-compliance
Lightning Source LLC
LaVergne TN
LVHW010247110826
845151LV00004B/1414

* 9 7 8 1 4 2 5 5 2 3 0 3 9 *